LIVING LOVED

Awakening Your Heart To The Father's Love

Ryan Bruss

Copyright © 2020 Ryan Bruss
All rights reserved.
ISBN: 9798649433419

Unless otherwise indicated, all Scripture quotations are taken from the New King James Version®. Copyright © 1982 by Thomas Nelson. Used by permission. All rights reserved.

DEDICATION

This book is dedicated to all those who desire a deeper love relationship with Father God. My prayer is that through this book, your heart will be awakened to the love of the Father like never before.

"[T]hat He would grant you, according to the riches of His glory, to be strengthened with might through His Spirit in the inner man, that Christ may dwell in your hearts through faith; that you, being rooted and grounded in love, may be able to comprehend with all the saints what is the width and length and depth and height—to know the love of Christ which passes knowledge; that you may be filled with all the fullness of God." Ephesians 3:16-19

LIVING LOVED

ACKNOWLEDGEMENTS

A special thank you to all the men and women of God who I have been privileged to study through the years to help me draw closer to the Father heart of God. Some of these beloved saints have left this earth and are now enjoying the fullness of the Father's love in Heaven. Thank you to my wife, Megan, for supporting me as I locked myself away to write this book. Thank you to Crystal Harden for all the effort you put into proofreading and editing. Thank you to Tracy at *Virtually Possible Designs* for another great cover. Thank you to Dr. Kevin Zadai for writing the introduction from your own encounter with the Father's love. Your teachings have changed my life. A special thank you to John Arnott for your endorsement. You are a truly carrier of the Father's heart. Thank you to all those who call Antioch Community Church your home—love you all!

And of course, thank you, Father God, for awakening my heart to the joy of living loved every day.

LIVING LOVED

CONTENTS

	Introduction	9
1	You Are Loved	13
2	Journey Of Awakening	33
3	Song Of All Songs	47
4	Roses And Lilies	57
5	A Lily Among Thorns	69
6	Enjoying God	75
7	The Banqueting House	87
8	Lovesick	99
9	The Hands of Father	117
10	Please Leave Me Alone	125
11	Leaping and Skipping	133

12	Gazing	143
13	Come Away	151
14	A New Season	157
15	The Secret Place of His Love	167
16	Little Foxes	179
17	Awakened To Love	185
18	Sitting At The Feet Of Jesus	201
19	Promises And Declarations	211

INTRODUCTION

I remember being shown the love of our Father God when I was on the other side. I was shown how that the Majestic Trinity met and decided to make man. As they discussed the details, they agreed to make man in their own image. The Holy Trinity wanted fellowship with their man, so they created this beautiful place called earth and placed the man and the woman in Eden. However, the biggest risk in creating man in their image was the liability that occurs when free will is involved. The Trinity discussed this liability and knew that man would disobey and fall. Even though God does not allow His foreknowledge to influence our free will, He can make provision for us because of His love for us. Jesus was chosen before the foundation of the world to be that provision. The fact that man fell did not surprise God at all. We have been given the gift of repentance in order to turn toward God's perfect will for our lives. God is so good that that goodness leads us to repentance. Romans 2:4 clearly says, *"Or despisest thou the riches of his goodness and forbearance and longsuffering; not knowing that the goodness of God leadeth thee to repentance?" (KJV)*

Jesus was the exact representation of the Father and displayed His Father's heart on the earth during His life and ministry. He bought back every human being so that total restoration could occur between God and man. The manifest Son of God went around doing good and healing everyone that was oppressed of the devil (see Acts 10:38).

Jesus recently expressed to me in a visitation that He and the Father love people, and they are not doing the terrible things that are occurring on the earth. He said that the "god of this world, Satan, is doing these wicked things and slandering God Almighty. Jesus then asked me to defend them before the people of the earth by preaching the good news of the gospel. We are to have a passionate love for God for His goodness toward us and not blame Him for the fallen state of this world. We need to accept the love of the Father and be overtaken by His goodness daily. Remember when you first were born again, the love you experienced. It is time to yield to the Spirit and do the mighty works that God ordained for you to walk in as His child. We are one day going to be in Paradise, restored back to the perfect will of God. Jesus is calling us back to our first love.

> *Revelation 2:4-7 says, "But I have this against you: you have abandoned the passionate love you had for me at the beginning. Think about how far you have fallen! Repent and do the works of love you did at first. I will come to you and remove your lampstand from its place of influence if you do not repent. Although, to your credit, you despise the practices of the Nicolaitans, which I also despise. The one whose heart is open let him listen carefully to what the Spirit is saying now to all the churches. To the one who overcomes I will give access to feast on the fruit of the Tree of Life that is found in the paradise of God." TPT*

Please, do not let anything delay you from entering into the perfect love of God and receiving your inheritance. You have so much value to the Holy Trinity. Let the Holy Spirit minister to you as my friend, Ryan Bruss, reveals God's plan of love for you. You can finish your race with joy and receive your heavenly reward. Let the Father's heart manifest in your life, and become a history maker!

Dr. Kevin L. Zadai

Founder and President of Warrior Notes School of Ministry

1
YOU ARE LOVED

"God loves each of us as if there were only one of us."
Augustine

God is not withholding His love from you. He loves you. I mean, He really, really loves you. No matter what emotions that brings up within you, it doesn't change that fact that you are deeply loved and adored by Father God. He loves you with a joyful, deep and everlasting love. By the time you are done reading this book, I believe those first couple of sentences will mean something vastly different to you than they do at this moment.

"...'Yes, I have loved you with an everlasting love; therefore with lovingkindness I have drawn you.'" Jeremiah 31:3b

Several years ago, I had a dream where a well-known prophet of God came to me, grabbed me by both of my shoulders, shook me, and said, "Live captivated by God!". That's how I want to live every day of my life—captivated. To be captivated by God is to daily run after His heart while enjoying His love, beauty, and presence.

At times, I can literally feel the beautiful, strong, tangible weight of His love on my heart. It is beyond any other feeling in the world, and I want you to experience the same. Father's love is meant to be felt, encountered, and enjoyed. With that being said, let me be the first one to remind us all that we do not go by how we feel. That's Christianity 101. However, I want to boldly tell you that you *can* literally feel the Father's love. As I write this, I can feel His love falling on me like a soft blanket. It's wonderful, and I pray that you feel the same thing right now!

However, I need you to understand from the very beginning of this book that is not about *always feeling* Father's love. There are many times in my own life where if I just stop and think about His love for me and those around me, my heart becomes exhilarated and full of joy. It's not because I necessarily *feel* the love of the Father at that moment, but I just know that I know that I know that He loves us beyond measure. I simply have the revelation that I am His son, and He loves me and believes in me, even in my weaknesses and shortcomings.

Friend, it's not about being perfect to live loved by God (more on that later); it's about knowing how strong His love is for us even when we fail. I believe in repentance with all of my heart. I repent all the time. I want to keep short accounts with the Lord, as I don't want anything standing in the way between me and the Father. I don't want anything hindering the relationship that we have together, so I want to keep my own life pure and clean before Him. Remember that God's love covers a multitude of sins (see 1 Peter 4:8) when we seek His forgiveness and choose to live pure in His sight.

So, right now, I'm believing that even in these opening paragraphs, you are beginning to feel different on the inside. I am believing that you are beginning to feel the tug of the Holy Spirit as He draws you closer to the Father heart of God. I want you to live loved!

"God loved us before He made us; and his love has never diminished and never shall." Julian of Norwich

YOU WANT TO BE LOVED

Now, it doesn't matter who you are, how you were raised or what has happened to you in your life, you want to be loved. And I'm not talking about some kind of superficial love, but a love that knows every last little thing about you, yet remains powerful and unshaken. This is the Father's love.

Love, the God kind of love, is the central and eternal theme of the entire Word of God.

"For God so loved the world..." John 3:16

Here's the problem: it's one thing to talk about Father's love, yet it's an entirely different thing to live loved—to live daily feeling the sweet and strong embrace of Abba's love. Sometimes I like to refer to Father God as "Abba", which is an Aramaic word meaning "Father". It's simply another way to express a term of endearment to God by referring to Him as our "Abba".

"And because you are sons, God has sent forth the Spirit of His Son into your hearts, crying out, 'Abba, Father!'" Galatians 4:6

Beloved, you belong to Abba. You are not an orphan; you are a son or a daughter. And to live in the revelation that Father loves, desires, adores, and enjoys you is the greatest privilege in all the world. The problem that I find with many, many Christians is that they do not know how to live like Father's beloved child. They live as orphans with orphan spirits.

It has now been over 34 years since my dad went to be with Jesus. I was at the tender age of 12 when he died of cancer, and he had been sick for five years before that. So, from the ages of 7 to 12, I really didn't get to know my father very well. Friends, life on earth is not easy or fair sometimes.

If you knew me personally, you would know that I share much about the Father heart of God because of what He has done in my own heart through the years. Yes, I still miss my dad, and I will see him again one day. However, the "sting" of his death that once overwhelmed my heart has been replaced by Father's love. Memories of the loss are there, yes, but the sting is gone. And no matter what you have been through in life, the historical memory will never change—it happened. Good or bad—it happened. But what *can* change is the pain, regret, grief, shame, guilt and condemnation of the past! And this is done through the Father's love. Psalm 103:3 makes it abundantly clear that God forgives and heals EVERYTHING!

"Who forgives all your iniquities, who heals all your diseases" Psalm 103:3

Did you know that revelation doesn't change you? It's what you do with the revelation that changes you. You can read these opening pages and say, "I know that God loves me." And I believe you. I believe that you know that God loves you. But are you living in His love? To know that Father loves you is one thing. To receive His love and live your life out of His love is another matter entirely.

Most Christians will tell you that they believe that God loves them. However, when it gets down to it, they have trouble defining what His love looks and feels like. This is why many people in church today are still empty, lost, hurting, alone, grieving, falling into sin, broken, wounded, etc. They know theologically that Father loves them, but they do not know it experientially. Again, I tell you that Father's love is meant to be experienced and enjoyed. However, when you have a true revelation of the Father's love, you don't even have to *feel* anything to experience His love. That's right. You live in such confidence of His love that whether you actually tangibly feel His love or not does not change the fact that you know that you know He loves you with all of His heart. It's gazing into Father's heart by faith.

"Christians find it easier to believe that God exists than that God loves them." Brennan Manning

LOVE LANGUAGE

Love is God's first language. I want to help you know this love—the Father's love. I want to help you live loved. We are all on a journey to the center of the Father heart of God. My friend, Father loves you more than you will ever know in this life. What was once lost in the garden of Eden when Adam and Eve fell will be restored to you again one day in its fullness. Jesus has reconciled us back to the Father to bring us into fellowship once again.

As I said, each one of us is on a journey to the heart of God. It seems that for some, this journey is more difficult than others for various reasons that we will get to later. The truth is, everyone has the opportunity to be as close to Jesus as they want. Everyone has a divine opportunity to know the Father's love. We were created to live loved every single day and feel the embrace of our Father God.

The enemy certainly doesn't want you to have a revelation of Father's love, because the enemy knows that God's love changes everything. It changes the way you think about yourself. It changes the way you think about God. It changes the way you think about others. It changes everything! To receive and release the Father's love is one of the greatest privileges that we have as believers.

To know God's love is to know God. My hope and fervent prayer is that through this book, you will have a new understanding and revelation of how much Father loves and adores you at this very moment, right now...not in some future moment when you have your "act together". Right now, Jesus loves you with the full extent of His love. Right now, you are surrounded by His love. Here's the proof:

"[T]hat Christ may dwell in your hearts through faith; that you, being rooted and grounded in love, may be able to comprehend with all the saints what is the width and length and depth and height—to know the love of Christ which passes knowledge; that you may be filled with all the fullness of God." Ephesians 3:17-19

Did you catch that? Right now, Jesus is dwelling in your heart through faith so that you are able to know that you know that He loves you. Do you believe this? It's the Word of the Lord to you. But it's your choice if you are going to believe it or not. No matter what your heart may feel like right now, you are literally surrounded by His love. Believing that God loves you first comes by faith in His Word about you. You have to come to Him by faith, believing that you are loved, that you are His favorite and that He rewards those who run after His heart.

"But without faith it is impossible to please Him, for he who comes to God must believe that He is, and that He is a rewarder of those who diligently seek Him." Hebrews 11:6

AFTER GOD'S OWN HEART

One of my favorite people to study in the Bible is King David. He lived as one who truly knew the great joy and pleasure of living as God's beloved. And He knew this before he even became king. David would pen beautiful thoughts from his heart like this:

"But I am poor and needy; yet the Lord thinks upon me. You are my help and my deliverer; do not delay, O my God." Psalm 40:17

Who says things like that? I am poor and I am needy, but you, Lord, are always thinking about me. I am always on your heart and mind! Those who know the Father can write the words that flow from the Father's heart.

David cultivated his love for God when he was faithfully and diligently tending sheep. David was developing his heart for God, receiving revelation of the heart of God and encountering the richness of God's love all while working a full-time job. Did you know that you can work a full-time job and live passionately in love with God at the same time? When you learn to cultivate a heart for God in private, you will encounter His love in public. And when you live full of God everywhere you go, many, many people will be affected because of the overflow of His presence in your life. Love is meant to be received and given away.

That's what I love about the life of David. Just read the Psalms again for yourself, and your heart will be exhilarated with all the wonderful thoughts that God has toward you. Read and meditate on this passage from Psalm 139, and allow the Holy Spirit to awaken the truths within you at this moment:

"O Lord, You have searched me and known me. You know my sitting down and my rising up; You understand my thought afar off. You comprehend my path and my lying down, and are acquainted with all my ways.

For there is not a word on my tongue, but behold, O Lord, You know it altogether. You have hedged me behind and before, and laid Your hand upon me. Such knowledge is too wonderful for me; it is high, I cannot attain it.

Where can I go from Your Spirit? Or where can I flee from Your presence? If I ascend into heaven, You are there; if I make my bed in hell, behold, You are there. If I take the wings of the morning, and dwell in the uttermost parts of the sea, even there Your hand shall lead me, and Your right hand shall hold me. If I say, 'Surely the darkness shall fall on me,' even the night shall be light about me; indeed, the darkness shall not hide from You, but the night shines as the day; the darkness and the light are both alike to You.

For You formed my inward parts; you covered me in my mother's womb. I will praise You, for I am fearfully and wonderfully made; marvelous are Your works, and that my soul knows very well. My frame was not hidden from You, when I was made in secret, and skillfully wrought in the lowest parts of the earth.

Your eyes saw my substance, being yet unformed. And in Your book they all were written, the days fashioned for me, when as yet there were none of them. How precious also are Your thoughts to me, O God! How great is the sum of them! If I should count them, they would be more in number than the sand..." Psalm 139:1-18

As you read in this Psalm, God thinks incredible thoughts about you. You may not have many good thoughts about yourself right now, but God has many, many wonderful thoughts about you. If Jesus appeared to you right now and began to tell you what He *really* thinks about you, you would weep and rejoice at the same time. Why? It would feel and seem too good to be true! If you learn to be quiet and still before God, you will hear those wonderful thoughts about yourself from the Father. And once you hear and receive those thoughts and allow them to become your identity, your life will radically change. If your identity (how you live, think, and feel about yourself every day) does not line up with what Father feels about you, then things need to change.

David lived knowing that God took great delight in him. Listen to what he said in Psalm 18:

"He delivered me because He delighted in me." Psalm 18:19b

That's a man who knew God's love. Will you just take a moment and meditate on the previous verse? Find a place to get alone with God, and read the verse again, and thank the Lord that He is going to deliver you because He delights in you—because He loves you. Let His waves of love and joy wash over your heart and bring you peace and healing, knowing that He delights in you! You! He delights in you, my friend! He takes great pleasure in you, and He loves you so much. You are His favorite, but you have to let these truths sink deep into your heart right now. God means what He says, and He says what He means. When God says that He takes great delight in you, He does take great delight in you.

"They looked to Him and were radiant, and their faces were not ashamed." Psalm 34:5

You see, when we look at Jesus, we become radiant, because He changes us from the inside out. God's love moves us from mundane living to a life filled with supernatural encounters. We have to be persistent and diligent in our pursuit of His love. We don't ever give up, but we keep asking, seeking and knocking. And if we do that, we will discover His love and experience the depths of His heart.

I want to live radiant as I look to Him. How about you? I'm after living in the pleasure of God, even in the mundane moments of my life, feeling His love and living daily in His presence. King David knew how to do just that: live daily in God's presence. Even when David sinned greatly, he knew how to repent and get his heart right before God. He knew that he knew that God loved him and was for him, even in his sin and weakness.

Have you ever wondered why we read that when King Saul sinned, God removed him from his place as king, but when David sinned, God forgave him, and David kept his throne? It was a matter of the heart. You see, the Bible says that Saul was the choice of the people (see 1 Samuel 12:13), but David was the choice of God.

"And Samuel said to Saul, 'You have done foolishly. You have not kept the commandment of the Lord your God, which He commanded you. For now the Lord would have established your kingdom over Israel forever. But now your kingdom shall not continue. The Lord has sought for Himself a man after His own heart, and the Lord has commanded him to be commander over His people, because you have not kept what the Lord commanded you.'" 1 Samuel 13:13-14

David's heart was not perfect, as we know, but it was pure before God. And God really loved that about David. You are a person after God's own heart. Did you know that? You say, "Ryan, you don't know what I have done. You don't know what has been done to me. You don't know what I have been through." And you're right; I don't know those things. But if God can call David a man after God's own heart, if God can trust a former murder—Paul the Apostle—with the Gospel, then surely God's love is deep enough to love you and me.

"There is no pit so deep that God's love is not deeper still." Corrie Ten Boom

As I have already taught you, right now, you are surrounded by God's love. It's not always about feeling, as I said; it's about having the faith in God to believe and receive that you are His beloved. One of the biggest hindrances to people experiencing God's love is that they are not good receivers. We have to learn to *receive* His love. We have to receive His love into our past. We have to receive His love into our present. And we have to receive His love into our future. His love changes everything. Father God is filled with inexpressible hope and joy for your future.

Many times, as I have taught on the Father's love, I have felt His presence so strong, and I pray that as you are reading this book, you are feeling the presence of God. I pray that you would literally feel Father God's love and tender heart toward you as you continue to read this book. If you will put into practice the principles contained within this book, you will experience the Father's embrace. Let Him love on you even now. Let Him heal your heart so you can live overflowing with this love.

"You will show me the path of life; in Your presence is fullness of joy; at Your right hand are pleasures forevermore." Psalm 16:11

That's one of my favorite verses in the entire Bible, because it shows us that there is a path to God's heart. There's a path to knowing His love, His power, His goodness, His kindness, and His joy. This book will help you get on the right path to begin to know God's heart for you. This book will teach you how to live loved.

In His presence is fullness of joy. You need His presence. You need His love to fill every part of your heart. This world can be so cruel and wicked, and if we don't stay close to Father's heart, this world will inevitably affect us. Our hearts must be guarded with the Father's love. Our hearts must be filled with the Father's love every single day. We need to live loved!

My friend, the truth is, when you draw near to God, He always draws near to you (see James 4:7-8). Always.

SONS AND DAUGHTERS

Because of a lack of teaching and understanding of the Father heart of God, many live as slaves in fear, rather than sons and daughters of a loving Father. It is one of the enemy's favorite deceptions. The enemy knows that you are saved, but he will do ALL that he can to make you feel distant from God like a slave with no rights, privileges or love. It's a "just obey and do" mentality. The enemy wants you to live like a slave in Egypt—with all of its fears and bondages, rather than enjoying fellowship with the Father in the Promised Land.

"For as many as are led by the Spirit of God, these are sons of God. For you did not receive the spirit of bondage again to fear, but you received the Spirit of adoption by whom we cry out, 'Abba, Father.' The Spirit Himself bears witness with our spirit that we are children of God, and if children, then heirs—heirs of God and joint heirs with Christ, if indeed we suffer with Him, that we may also be glorified together." Romans 8:14-17

You see, when we don't understand sonship (when I use the word sonship, I am referring to both men and women, of course), which is the beauty of being loved, cherished and adored by Abba, then we will live in fear. And that binds our hearts so that we are not able to receive and give love to our wonderful Father.

Many people in church today still have not grasped the fact that they are sons and daughters of God—not slaves—not orphans—not second class citizens. These same people feel that Father has been very disappointed in them through the years, because they have been so disappointed in themselves. And when we do not have a healthy view of

Father God, we will live feeling that we are continually falling short of Father loving us with all of His heart.

Some people even feel that Father has abandoned them through the years. They feel like Father God is crabby, annoyed and a distant grouch that simply tolerates us until we see Him in Heaven one day.

How do you feel that Father sees you? How do you feel He thinks about you? Think about it for a moment right now: "How do I feel that Father sees me?" Those thoughts that come to your mind—those emotions you are feeling—you are living from that place in your life right now.

Daily, we live our lives based on what we are experiencing at any given moment within our hearts. Think about it: When you're happy or joyful within, how do you live? How do you relate to people and the world around you? If you are sad, hurt or grieved within your heart, how do you interact with people throughout the day? Sure, anyone can put on a front or mask their feelings, but that doesn't change what is taking place within a person's heart. And Father is after your heart. He's after your soul—your mind, will and emotions.

You see, if you are born again, your spirit is alive on the inside! You are carrying the Kingdom of God within you.

"For indeed, the kingdom of God is within you." Luke 17:21b

Because the kingdom of God is within you, great joy, peace, love and everything you need is also within you! (I cover this in detail in my book, *Carrying the Presence*.) However, if we have not learned to allow the Holy Spirit to deal with the soulish part of our lives (again, the mind, will and emotions), we will never fully encounter God like we desire. I pray that this book will not only bring revelation of Father's love for you, but it will also break down barriers, remove hindrances and provide a supernatural pathway for you to encounter God like never before!

There are things in each of our lives that need to be dealt with if we are going to experience more and more of Him. I don't know about you, but I have a longing for more. I want to know more about Jesus today than I knew yesterday.

Intimacy with God is our spiritual life source. When we spend time with our Father, it awakens within us the possibilities of all that we may encounter in Him. Everything that the Bible says we can have...we can have. But most things we receive from God come to us out of relationship with God, not religion or religious activities. I believe that the launching pad for experiencing God in ways that we have always desired begins with the revelation that we are loved, adored, and cherished by the God of the universe, Abba, Father.

"God proved His love on the Cross. When Christ hung, and bled, and died, it was God saying to the world, 'I love you.'"
Billy Graham

Living Loved

2
JOURNEY OF AWAKENING

"The Christian experience, from start to finish, is a journey of faith." Watchman Nee

We are all on a spiritual journey. Let me tell you a little bit about my journey of awakening to know God's love. As I mentioned earlier, when I was only seven years old, my family found out that my dad had cancer. He was sick for five years and died when I was only twelve. My whole family was saved, and we loved the Lord, but cancer came into our home and took my father. My mom had to raise us three children without a husband, and it was very difficult, as you can imagine. You may have experienced something like this in your own life or perhaps something much worse. I never try to compare what I have gone through with what someone else has gone through, because we all respond to negative life circumstances differently. I'm just giving you a snapshot of my own life as an example of one person's journey into the Father heart of God.

As a teenager, I had bottled up the emotions of my dad's death. Being the oldest of three kids, I wanted to try to be the man of the house, and obviously, that was not what I was supposed to be doing. Nor did my own mother put that pressure on me; I put that pressure on myself. When I was a teenager, the enemy tried to draw me away from God through the things of this world. That is, until a prophet came to town when I was eighteen, and at a church meeting, he had me stand up in front of everybody and prophesied hope and a future over my wounded heart.

No matter what you are facing right now in your own life, Father has a bright future mapped out for you. Father's heart is bursting with this truth about you:

"For I know the thoughts that I think toward you, says the LORD, thoughts of peace and not of evil, to give you a future and a hope. Then you will call upon Me and go and pray to Me, and I will listen to you. And you will seek Me and find Me, when you search for Me with all your heart." Jeremiah 29:11-13

That prophetic word over my life was one of the most extraordinary things that has ever happened to me. From that moment on, I decided that I wanted to serve the Lord with all my heart for the rest of my life.

However, in my early twenties, I struggled to know God's love. In my mind, I knew that He loved me, but in my heart, I could not seem to receive His love. It was very frustrating for me, because I'm a very feeling person. I wanted to feel His love. I didn't want to just talk about His love, I wanted to *know* His love and experience it for myself. I grew tired of just reading and hearing about God's love without experiencing it for myself.

What I am about to share with you changed my life forever, and I know that it will do the same for you if you simply put these truths into practice. I started reading every book I could find on the Father's love. I wanted to understand His love, but I needed a revelation. For hours and hours, I studied and read the Word of God, searching for His love. I diligently studied the Song of Songs (or Song of Solomon). I studied all the places where Jesus talked about love. I studied where God the Father talked about love. I studied the Epistles that taught on God's love. I dove headfirst into studying the emotions of God through the Psalms and the life of David. I literally meditated day and night on the love of God. My passionate desire to know His love for myself far outweighed the journey it took to get there. All of a sudden, something fascinating began to happen to me. The more I studied, prayed, meditated, fasted, and worshipped, the hungrier I became to know Father's love.

You see, Father's love had to heal my heart and break through my spirits of abandonment, shame, fatherlessness, discouragement and so on from growing up without a father. When traumatic things happen in our lives, we tend to project the hurt and disappointment onto God. For instance, I felt that my earthly father abandoned me, in a sense, when he died, so my heart felt that my heavenly Father would also abandon me when I needed Him most. My dad was not there when I needed someone to talk to, so I felt that God would not be there when I needed someone to talk to. You get the picture.

These are hindrances that keep us from experiencing the depth of Father's love for us. You may have grown up in an abusive home, or maybe one of your parents was an alcoholic, or maybe you had a great father, but there is something in you that just has trouble receiving love. Whatever the case may be, I'm talking about this moment right here, right now—you can live loved. You can literally live loved every single day and encounter the embrace of Father God. So I studied as much as I could, and I prayed and prayed and worshipped and prayed some more until everything I was reading and studying became a reality in my life as my heart was healed and I received His love deep within my heart. All that hard work of studying, repenting, talking to God, learning, growing, and renewing my mind with what God really thought about me deeply impacted me. My very identity was renewed from one that could not receive the Father's love to a man that lived loved. I then began to daily live loved as my identity had become rooted and grounded in the love of the Father.

Did you know that in the book of John, the apostle John wrote on five different occasions that he was the one that Jesus loved (John 13:23; 19:26; 20:2; 21:7 & 20)? John had a divine revelation of how much Jesus loved him. I love that he defined himself as the one that Jesus loved, and after you read this book you will be doing the same thing. With confidence, you will say, "I'm the one that Jesus loves!"

All of the studying, praying, worshipping, and meditating on the goodness and love of God filled my heart to overflowing. Remember, during that season of diligently seeking to know His heart, I was, of course, born-again. I really loved the Lord, but I had to learn to remove the hindrances to receiving His love so I could *live loved*. I needed to have the revelation that His banner over me truly was love (I teach on His banner of love later in this book). I had to learn that Jesus has already done everything He needs to do for me and that it was my heart that needed a change. It was my thoughts that needed to change, not God's thoughts. Once I absorbed this revelation into my spirit when I was in my early twenties (I'm now in my late forties as of this writing), I have felt loved by God ever since. There is no doubt within me that God loves me and that He is for me. And I don't want you to ever doubt again that Father loves you deeply.

Incidentally, the length of the process that I'm talking about where I began to *live loved* will vary from person to person. For some, it may take days, weeks, or months, as this has to be walked out every day. For others, the process may take longer because of all the things that have happened in the life of that individual. Some people are better "receivers" than others, so it doesn't take as long to learn to live loved once the truths are applied to their lives. Some people have to let go of the shame, regret, guilt and condemnation that

When we are born again, we go from darkness to light (see 1 Peter 2:9), and our spirit is made new (2 Corinthians 5:17). However, this soulish realm, our mind, will and emotions, still has to go through the process of being healed, cleansed, renewed and set free, as there are many things that we have gone through in life where we need to forgive others, forgive ourselves, let go of regret, give our pasts to God, and the list goes on. This inner turmoil that people face is what is hindering them from experiencing the Father's love and embrace in greater dimensions.

Some people have gone through so much in their lives that they don't even know who they really are in the deepest places of their heart. Are you one of those people? Father's love is for you. Please don't let the fact that those hidden areas of your heart feel too painful to yield to God, or that you feel it's too much work to take care of business within your heart, keep you from experiencing Father's love. And don't let pride get in the way of receiving Father's love. You don't want to get to the end of your life and look back and think, "What was I doing? It wasn't worth hanging on to all the junk. I should have just yielded to the healing love of God."

"Is it a small thing in your eyes to be loved by God—to be the son, the spouse, the love, the delight of the King of glory? Christian, believe this, and think about it: you will be eternally embraced in the arms of the love which was from everlasting, and will extend to everlasting—of the love which brought the Son of God's love from heaven to earth, from earth to the

cross, from the cross to the grave, from the grave to glory— that love which was weary, hungry, tempted, scorned, scourged, buffeted, spat upon, crucified, pierced—which fasted, prayed, taught, healed, wept, sweated, bled, died. That love will eternally embrace you." Richard Baxter

One of my greatest passions in life is to help you become untethered from anything and everything that is causing you to live any less than daily experiencing the depths of Father's love for you—to help you remove all hinderances to love, receive healing and live loved every day.

What is keeping *you* from experiencing His great love? Those who know you and spend time with you will know if you are living loved by Father, because it changes the way we live. The fruit of love blossoms from a heart that is in love, and people can sense that. What are some of the fruits of love? Read the list:

"Love suffers long and is kind; love does not envy; love does not parade itself, is not puffed up; does not behave rudely, does not seek its own, is not provoked, thinks no evil; does not rejoice in iniquity, but rejoices in the truth; bears all things, believes all things, hopes all things, endures all things. Love never fails..." 1 Corinthians 13:4-8

What is keeping you from experiencing His love? To whatever level you have experienced His love, there is an infinite amount more still to be discovered, because you will never exhaust Father's supply of love. Father's love—it's so rich, so heartwarming, so healing, so good, so tangible, so exhilarating that just a "thimble full" of it can satisfy a broken, cold, lonely, and distant heart. So, what is keeping you from personally experiencing Father's love to the point that you can say with confidence, "I am living loved!"?

Is it your upbringing? His love will set you free from every negative emotion from all that you have been through. Is it past failures, regrets, and sins? All of us have a past—all of us. The historical memory of what you have done or been through may not change, but the negative emotions attached to that memory will change by His love and forgiveness. The blood of Jesus is what cleanses us and releases us from our past so we can encounter Father's love.

We know ourselves better than anyone else, and we sometimes feel that because God has the same information about us that we have, there is no way that He can love us so deeply. So, instead of running to Him as a little child, we tend to try to "hide" from God, close ourselves off from His love and even the love of those around us, further distancing our hearts from Him.

What is keeping you from receiving Father's love? Maybe you have absorbed bad theology through the years about God's love for you. If that's you, your theology is about to change for the good. Maybe you feel like you missed God at some point in your life. My friend, if you are still breathing, there is still time to encounter Father's love. The book of your life is still being written; you're not at the end of your story!

Father God never, ever quits on us. We quit on us, others quit on us, but God never quits on us! Now that's good news! You are going to learn so much from this book. I believe that when we get into the Song of Songs in the next chapter, your entire paradigm of God's love will change.

"Do you believe that the God of Jesus loves you beyond worthiness and unworthiness, beyond fidelity and infidelity—that he loves you in the morning sun and in the evening rain—that he loves you when your intellect denies it, your emotions refuse it, your whole being rejects it. Do you believe that God loves without condition or reservation and loves you this moment as you are and not as you should be?"
Brennan Manning, All Is Grace: A Ragamuffin Memoir

PERSONAL APPLICATION

Right now, you are on your own personal journey of awakening to know God's heart for you. So, where can you start at this moment before we move on?

1. Find yourself a quiet place, and express your love to God through worship and prayer.

2. Ask the Holy Spirit who searches hearts to show you all that is hindering you from receiving more of His love. Be still, and see what He brings to your heart. In the space provided, write down those areas in your life that you feel are hindering you from receiving the love of God. It could be the way you were raised, trauma that you have been through, past sins and failures, etc. Whatever the case may be, it's good to write them down so you can feel a release in your heart. Again, ask the Holy Spirit to show you these sometimes buried and hidden areas:

_____
_____
_____
_____
_____
_____
_____
_____
_____
_____
_____

_____
_____
_____
_____
_____
_____

3. Forgive others, ask for forgiveness from God and forgive yourself. Receive healing into your heart. Is there someone you need to forgive? Ask the Holy Spirit to bring names to your remembrance. Write those names here:

_____
_____
_____
_____
_____
_____
_____
_____

4. Begin to receive His love, and embrace it by faith. Remember, you don't always feel something. Sometimes it's a beautiful, quiet knowing that He is with you, and He loves you. This is a great place to start—the assurance of His love. Take some of your favorite Bible verses about Father's love (you can find them throughout this book), and meditate on those precious truths. You can also use some of the phrases that I put together for you in chapter eighteen to commune with God. Whatever you do, take your time, and enjoy the

process with the Lord. Write down a few of your favorite verses about God's love to meditate on over and over:

_____
_____
_____
_____
_____
_____
_____
_____
_____
_____
_____
_____
_____
_____
_____
_____
_____
_____

5. Begin to live loved!

3

SONG OF ALL SONGS

"I am my beloved's, and my beloved is mine..." Song of Songs 6:3

My friend, what I am about to share with you in these next few chapters has completely changed my life, and I pray that it changes your life as well.

For some reason, many Christians do not read the Song of Solomon or what is also known as the Song of Songs. In this book, I'm going to call it the Song of Songs. This small book of the Bible is truly the Song of ALL Songs. It's Father's love letter to His children that maps out our journey of love with Jesus.

One day, I was sitting at my desk in my home office studying this Song, and the glory of the Lord came into the room and visited me. The entire room filled with the presence of God. It was so strong, so real, and so tangible that I could hardly stand it. It was as if the Lord was revealing to me that I was on the right track, studying His heart and receiving fresh insights of His love through this amazing book of the Bible. My prayer for you is that as you read this book and meditate on Father's love for you found in the Song of Songs, you will also feel the very atmosphere of Heaven fill the place where you're reading, and you will experience the presence of God like you never have before.

Psalm 16:11, "You will show me the path of life; in Your presence is fullness of joy; at Your right hand are pleasures forevermore."

The Song of Songs is more than a "book" of the Bible—it is a Song—and a love song at that. It is eight glorious chapters of insight into the heart of God. It is your guidebook to help you encounter the love of God in different seasons of your life.

Reading, encountering, and meditating on this Song will deepen and strengthen your intimate walk with God. It's for everyone—every woman AND every man! These days, men especially need a revelation of the heart of God—a revelation of the Father's heart. Men, studying this Song will strengthen your heart to give love and to receive love—love *for* God, love *from* God, love for others and love for yourself. Yes, this Song is a journey in love.

The more I study this Song, the more it awakens my heart, and the more deeply I fall in love with Jesus. There is such power in this Song—the power to change your life forever. Take this Song verse by verse, and pray and meditate over it.

Cross-reference it with other verses. Study commentaries, and read the tremendous insights that others have discovered. Pray the verses back to God, and see yourself in the love story. Take your time with it, don't be in a hurry, and don't give up. It is so worth the time and effort.

It is also essential that we study and encounter this Song for the coming days ahead. Those whose hearts are rooted and grounded in Father's love will survive even the darkest of times. Nothing can shake or shatter a heart that has its roots deep in the Father's love.

Since my early days of encountering the Father's love, I have already faced, as the song Amazing Grace says:

"...many dangers, toils and snares I have already come; 'Tis Grace that brought me safe thus far and Grace will lead me home."

And I have lived out this verse many times over as well:

"Many are the afflictions of the righteous, but the LORD delivers him out of them all." Psalm 34:19

But His love has been my anchor. His love has been my sure foundation. His love has brought me through. At one of the lowest points in my Christian walk, I remember walking back and forth in my bedroom, longing to hear God's voice. This was not about if He still loved me. I just wanted to hear Him in my darkest hour. Still walking back and forth, all of a sudden, I heard this verse come up in my spirit, pushing through the dark hour:

"If I make my bed in hell, behold, You are there." Psalm 139:8b

Friends, His love remains steadfast and unchanging, even in our darkest hour. What love!

"Through the LORD's mercies we are not consumed, because His compassions fail not. They are new every morning; great is Your faithfulness." Lamentations 3:22-23

As you embark on this beautiful journey with me into the heart of God, you will not be disappointed, because Father's love does not disappoint.

THE SHULAMITE AND HER BELOVED

This entire book, the Song of Songs, is a story of the journey of a young woman (the Shulamite) to find the one that she loves (her Beloved). Within this short book, you will find some of the most incredible teachings on God's love for us—more than anywhere else in the Bible.

Although this love story is a literal interpretation about this young woman being wooed by King Solomon, it can also be interpreted as the beautiful love song of the relationship between Jesus and each one of His sons and daughters. It's a journey of spiritual maturity in our love relationship with

Jesus. This Song is for every man, woman, and child. Again, the truths within this Song will change your life forever if you allow your heart to be open to receive the good things that God has for you through this beautiful Song of all Songs. In this book, I have chosen to share out of Song of Songs chapter two.

When we first come to know Jesus through the born again experience, we love Him, of course, but it is weak love. Our love for Jesus has to continually mature as we travel through this life hand in hand with our Messiah. It's the same thing when you get married. When you fall in love with someone and get married, as intimate and exciting as that new love is, their love is still immature because it has not stood the test of time. It is sincere love. It is true love. But it is immature love. A couple that stays in love and matures in love through all the ups and downs will grow stronger and stronger, not weaker.

In our relationship with Jesus, we want to mature in our love for Him. When we are born again, our love for Jesus is exciting and raw, real and authentic, and we want to continue to fan that flame of love within our hearts until it becomes a blazing fire of love and passion for the One who gave us His life.

"Incomprehensible and immutable is the love of God. For it was not after we were reconciled to Him by the blood of His Son that He began to love us, but He loved us before the foundation of the world, that with His only begotten Son we

*too might be sons of God before we were anything at all."
Augustine*

As you take the journey with me in just one of the chapters in the Song of Songs, you will begin to see how absolutely wonderful and exhilarating it is to live loved. Jesus is beautiful and full of mercy. He is the kindest person you will ever meet. He is unbelievably patient with us. Jesus is the greatest thing that has ever happened to us, and if we really begin to know Him for who He is and how He feels about us, we will live our lives in an entirely different way.

You see, Jesus believes in you like no one else does. He sees the depths of your heart, every weakness, and all of the immaturity, yet He loves you with all of His heart. I know that's hard to believe sometimes, because we feel that if people knew our shortcomings and failures, they would reject us—and we unconsciously do the same thing to Father God. He knows what we've been through. He knows what we've done, but He loves us the same. He does not reject us or distance Himself from us in our immaturity. If you ever feel distant from God, I want to tell you right now that it's nothing on God's end. It's on your end. It's something within your heart that needs to be healed, delivered, or changed. Remember, God doesn't just have love, He is love.

"...God is love." 1 John 4:8

Friend, God knows everything that you've been through...every heartache, every trial, every hurt, every pain.

He knows how you feel about Him right now. He knows how you feel about yourself, and He knows how you feel about others, yet He loves you so deeply and longs to hold you close on a regular basis. If you will learn to lean into His love like John the Beloved leaned on Jesus (see John 13:23), you will live loved.

There is a vast difference between a heart that is weak and immature, but desires to follow Jesus, and a heart that is outwardly saying all the right things and doing all the right things, but on the inside is rebellious and cold toward God.

I know you wouldn't be reading this book if you did not desire to fall in love with Jesus more and more. Intimacy with Jesus is a heart matter, plain and simple. Just look at all the people that God had compassion on throughout the Word of God, like David or the woman caught in adultery. Jesus loves a heart that is not rebellious. He's looking for the broken and contrite of heart. He's looking for hearts that are tender toward Him, because He will manifest Himself to those who have that kind of heart. But when a person's heart is cold and indifferent, hard and rebellious, He can't move in that person's life. But I know that's not your heart. I know that you love the Lord. I know that you desire to please Him. I know that you want live loved every day.

The Song of Songs is Father's love letter to His sons and daughters. When we see ourselves in the story, it begins to change our hearts into the way that He feels about us. When we have a revelation of God's heart for us, it changes every area of our lives, because we then filter everything through His love. It's the revelation of love that empowers us to live out the greatest commandments: to love God and to love others well. You have to always remember that everything—and I mean everything—flows out of love. Now, let's enjoy Song of Songs chapter two together.

"God is most glorified in us when we are most satisfied in Him." John Piper

PERSONAL APPLICATION

Take time to read and meditate on Song of Songs chapter two a few times. In the space provided, write down what the Holy Spirit showed you about Jesus. What did the Holy Spirit reveal to you about yourself? What did you feel in your heart? Let your heart flow as you write:

_____
_____
_____
_____
_____
_____
_____
_____
_____
_____
_____
_____
_____
_____
_____
_____
_____
_____
_____
_____
_____
_____
_____

Living Loved

4

ROSES AND LILIES

"I am the rose of Sharon, and the lily of the valleys."
Song of Songs 2:1

Contrary to popular belief, the rose of Sharon in Song of Songs chapter two, verse one is describing the young woman (or you and me), not Jesus. The rose and the lily described in this verse is for women as well as *men* to take hold of. I know that most men are not naturally inclined to see themselves as a fragrant flower like a rose or lily. If you're a guy reading this, you're going to have to put that to the side for now and understand what the Lord wants to show you here.

Maybe this illustration will help you men. Several years ago, I was replacing a section of brick on an old house. I had carried all the bricks to the side of the house. I mixed the mortar in a wheelbarrow, and brick by brick, I fixed a large whole in the house. It wasn't a large job, but enough to be tiring and plenty dirty. As I finished the job, I packed up all the tools and headed back to the work vehicle. As I gave the new brick job one last look, I looked behind me to make sure that I didn't leave any tools on the jobsite. It was then that I noticed that I had been four feet from the neighbor's beautiful rose bush all day, and I had never noticed it was there. I was so focused on my work that I never stopped to "smell the roses" or even notice them, for that matter. Before I left the jobsite, I took the time to enjoy their beauty and smell their fragrance. I have to tell you, it was very refreshing after doing brick work. Men, you are a rose before God...deal with it.

I will never forget the time that I taught on this verse to a group of pastors in Guatemala. I was able to give each one of them a rose as I taught the truths that you are also about to learn from this Scripture. I had a wonderful time watching their happy and somewhat confused faces as they each held their rose, but the life lessons they received caused them to carefully place the rose in their belongings so it wouldn't get crushed on the trip back to their villages.

What do *you* think of when you picture a rose? We have a rose bush growing in our backyard here in North Carolina, so I get to see them on a regular basis. And I would imagine that many of you have either given or received roses at some point in your life.

How many times have you stuck your nose into that bouquet of flowers and breathed in the intoxicating fragrance of the roses? It's a very distinct and refreshing smell that a rose gives off. In this verse, the woman is describing herself as the rose of Sharon. She sees her own heart like a rose with intoxicating beauty and fragrance before Jesus, no matter what she has been through or is going through at the moment. She is not declaring that her heart is mature or perfect, but neither is she declaring that her heart is rebellious or unclean, because a rebellious and unclean heart would not give off a fragrance that is a pleasing aroma to Jesus.

"Love and a red rose can't be hid." Thomas Holcroft

A heart that is pure and sincere in its love is like a beautiful and fragrant rose to Jesus (again both men and women). Have you ever seen yourself that way? You have to refuse to look at your past and even your present circumstances and take hold of the revelation that right now, you are like a rose before Him. Beauty is in the eye of the beholder, and you are the one that Father God is beholding.

In this verse, the Shulamite woman is boldly declaring, "I AM" the rose of Sharon. She's making a declaration that her identity is in the truth that she's a rose, no matter what the enemy has done to her, and no matter what other people think about her. My friend, you have to quit worrying about what others think about you. The truth is that you are fragrant and beautiful to God. Just like one of those roses in my backyard captures my heart, you have captured the heart of Jesus right now, right where you are at, and He loves you so much. You have captivated the heart of God.

You have to let this revelation sink deep—the revelation of how Jesus sees you and defines your beauty and worth. Jesus says, "You're worth it, you're beautiful, you're lovely to Me, you're My son, you're My daughter." And again, all you men out there, you are beautiful roses to Jesus, and you might as well just receive it!

As the Shulamite woman did, we all have to confess these, "I AM'S". Such as, "I AM the desire of God's heart. I AM loved by God. I AM beautiful to God. I AM the rose that Jesus longs for." She doesn't just say it; she declares it, "I AM!" (At the end of this book, I provided for you many verses that you can start declaring over your own life.) This is the point where the enemy will try to lie to you and say, "No, your heart is not lovely. It's weak and sinful. Your heart is not sincere. You don't love the Lord. You are not as special and beautiful to God as you think you are." These are all lies, and the enemy knows that the opposite of what he is saying to you is the truth! He's the father of lies (see John 8:44). When you hear that wicked accuser lie to you or try to remind you of your past, remind him that he's a liar, and there is NO TRUTH in him—and then receive the Father's love.

"'No weapon formed against you shall prosper, and every tongue which rises against you in judgment you shall condemn. This is the heritage of the servants of the LORD, and their righteousness is from Me,' says the LORD.'" Isaiah 54:17

LILY OF THE VALLEY

The Shulamite goes on to say that she is the lily of the valleys. The lily in this passage represents purity. We *can* live pure-hearted before God because of the power of forgiveness and the power of His blood. She is declaring that she is pure before God. She is saying, "I am a lily; I am pure-hearted. Devil, no matter what you would try to say to me, my heart is pure and sincere before God. My heart is not rebellious. I may be weak or immature at times, but my heart is still pure before Jesus." Men, once again, you are also pure-hearted lilies before God!

You see, lilies and roses do not have to pretend in anyway whatsoever. They are what they are. They are beautiful to behold and fragrant to the world. You don't have to pretend, either. Just receive the truth that you are beautiful and fragrant to God, and if those around you do not see the same worth in you, they can move along and find someone else to criticize. You may find this a bit amusing, but isn't it amazing how roses or lilies do not have to tell you they are beautiful or fragrant? They just are. Think about that when it comes to your own heart.

"Is not this lily pure? What fuller can procure [a] white so perfect, spotless clear [a]s in this flower doth appear?" Francis Quarles

Beloved, you have to see your heart has pure before God because of His abundant grace, mercy, and love. Because of the blood of Jesus, and because you've asked for forgiveness, you are pure before God. To not believe this as truth is like going into the shower, full of mud from head to toe, washing yourself clean, and then coming out of the shower feeling like you never even went in...when, in reality, you are clean from head to toe. You have to believe and receive the truth by faith that you are pure before God.

"Blessed are the pure in heart, for they shall see God." Matthew 5:8

We have to be careful that we don't have any hindrances to receiving Father's love into our hearts—hindrances like the false understanding that God receives us when we have not sinned and rejects us when we do sin. That is not how God's love manifests to us. Father's love is not fickle. I'm sure that the love you have for your kids is not like this—that if they do something good or right, you love them and hug them, but when they do something wrong, you reject them. No good and loving father or mother would treat their children like that. Through discipline, we still love and embrace our children, even when they do something wrong.

During the Christmas season, we like to buy an ornament for the Christmas tree as family. One particular year, when my kids were little, we decided on an ornament that was made of clay. It was a beautiful ornament that was a fireplace with stockings hung on the mantle. My son was particularly intrigued by the ornament when we brought it home. I made it clear to him several times to not touch it because of what it was made of and because it was fragile. About an hour later, I went into the room and saw the ornament on the table in a couple of pieces. I called Andrew in, and of course, he denied any wrongdoing. I asked again and again, and he kept denying that he did anything wrong. Finally, I said, "Andrew, I am not mad, but I have to know the truth. Did you break the ornament after I told you not to touch it?" He finally said yes. I took Him upstairs to his room and told him that he needed to ask God to forgive him for lying. Then he needed to ask my forgiveness for lying. I could see the weight lift off of him, because he knew that he had done wrong. And that's when I said, "I'm proud of you for asking for forgiveness, but now I am going to have to spank you." And I explained why. After the little spanking and a couple of crocodile tears on his end (and couple of crocodile tears in my own heart because of my deep love for him), we IMMEDIATELY hugged, and it couldn't have been any more than thirty seconds later that he was running around the house, full of joy again.

Yes, the Bible says that God disciplines those who He loves, and I've received much discipline! Otherwise, what kind of Father would He be? When you have a revelation of God's love, your entire paradigm of His discipline changes, because you then understand that His discipline leads to a greater depth of love and intimacy. I obviously did not discipline my son out of anger for what he did, but I disciplined him out of love—there's a big difference. When God brings correction into our life, it comes from His heart of love for us, and it's always for our good. Why did my son run around the house full of joy *soon after* I spanked him? Because Dad was not holding his past mistakes against him, and he knew that. He knew he did wrong. He repented and moved on in joy knowing that Dad's love for him was unmoved. It's the same with our Father in Heaven. When received, discipline from God will draw us closer to His heart and not farther away. So, you too, can run around the house in joy knowing that your sins are forgiven and that you are deeply loved by God!

Sin tries to wedge itself in between our relationship with God when we keep it hidden and unconfessed. But when we confess and repent of our sins, it's as if it never happened. The Bible is clear that confessed sin is washed away. He is such a good Father!

"If we confess our sins, He is faithful and just to forgive us our sins and to cleanse us from all unrighteousness." 1 John 1:9

You see, my friend, we have to quit assuming that Father's love is like human love. The way we love one another (or how we've been loved) and the way God loves us are two totally separate things. This is why we need a revelation of God's love—because you rarely find deep love on this earth. I'm talking about authentic, deep, pure, unconditional love. It's so rare on this earth, so we must go to God and His Word to receive a revelation of what love really looks and feels like. And then when we receive His love, we can demonstrate that same love to others.

We cannot define Father God's love by what we have negatively seen or experienced in the natural. We have to come to that place where internal love is defined by what Father thinks about us and nothing else. I don't know how many times over the years that I've laid my head on the pillow at night after a difficult day, whether something was my fault or someone else's, and I let Father's love wash over me. I let His perfect love define what happened to me in the day, focusing on how He feels about me, not what the circumstances look like.

You have to persevere and get to that place where love is more than a feeling. Again, it's the truth of God's Word that defines His love for us, so please quit being moved by what you feel about His love. Why do I say it like that? Because what you feel and what you are thinking could be at the other end of the spectrum from what God is feeling and thinking about you. If what you are feeling and thinking about God's love does not line up with the truth of His Word, it's not the love of the Father.

The young lady in our story says that she is the lily of the *valley.* The valley represents those low and dark places in this fallen world. Did you know that you can live pure in the midst of a dark valley? Did you know that you can live pure-hearted in the midst of a world that's full of sin? She declares that, "I am a lily—I am the pure-hearted one in the midst of a dark and sinful world." This expression of a person's heart is so precious to God, because in the midst of worldliness, we choose Jesus. We choose love. We choose to stay pure through the dark times and through the hard times. We choose to stay pure through the difficult times and through the pain and the suffering and all the temptations that we face.

She's not saying that her heart is perfect, but she's declaring that her heart is pure. She is the beautiful rose that intoxicates as it releases its fragrance, and she is the beautiful and pure lily in the midst of this world. Beloved, this is your heart as well!

"God only requires of his adult children, that their hearts be truly purified, and that they offer him continually the wishes and vows that naturally spring from perfect love. For these desires, being the genuine fruits of love, are the most perfect prayers that can spring from it. It is scarce conceivable how strait the way is wherein God leads them that follow him; and how dependent on him we must be, unless we are wanting in our faithfulness to him." John Wesley

PERSONAL APPLICATION

If you are able, why don't you buy a rose and/or lily, reread this chapter, and let the Holy Spirit speak to your heart again about your beauty, fragrance and worth? What is He speaking to your heart? In our story, the Shulamite woman declared, "I am the rose and the lily." You can also go to the end of this book and read the declarations provided for you and start declaring them over your own life. Are you beginning to receive His love? Are you beginning to understand your value before Father God? Write those thoughts here:

_____
_____
_____
_____
_____
_____
_____
_____
_____
_____
_____
_____
_____
_____
_____
_____
_____

Living Loved

5

A LILY AMONG THORNS

"Like a lily among thorns, so is my love among the daughters." Song of Songs 2:2

Now Jesus is speaking (the Beloved in our story). He calls her "my love". And He calls you *His love*. It's personal. Jesus is very personal with us. The thorns in this verse represent sin. Again, the valleys and the thorns do not define our relationship with God. Valleys and thorns are all around us, but they don't have to get into us. They do not define our walk with God.

Right now, Father sees you as a lily among thorns (again, thorns represent the sin of the world). He knows that there is sin all around you because you live in a fallen world. But in the midst of this fallen world, when He looks at you, He sees a pure-hearted lily. What a thought! Your heart for God stands out in the midst of all that is going on in the world around you. He sees the desire of your heart to live pure among the thorny places in this life. And Jesus declares over you, "I see your heart! I see the desire that you have within you to be pure and to love Me!"

As with the rose, the lily is also spectacular and breathtaking, captivating the very heart of Jesus. You captivate the heart of Jesus. We move the heart of God as we stand tall and beautiful in the midst of a sinful world. Do you remember how Jesus spoke of the lilies?

"Consider the lilies, how they grow: they neither toil nor spin; and yet I say to you, even Solomon in all his glory was not arrayed like one of these." Luke 12:27

King Solomon in all his glory couldn't even be compared to the beauty, worth and glory found in just one lily! And that's how Jesus sees you! When we really begin to understand and embrace how Jesus sees us, it changes everything. We find our identity and success in being desired by Jesus—not by what we do, but by *who we are.* The strength of our hearts must be rooted in His love and not in what we think about ourselves or what others think about us.

No matter what you have done or what you currently may be struggling with, the enemy has tried to define your life by all the low points—the valleys and the thorns. But not Jesus. When we have a revelation of how He sees our hearts, even in the midst of all our failures and successes, we will live loved.

You see, when we pass through the valley and the thorns, we must take every day to God and allow the revelation of His love to deepen within us, refusing to allow the valleys and thorns to define us. Valleys and thorns will come, but they do not have to define our walk with God. The Shulamite woman in these two verses is not declaring in her "I AM'S" that she is perfect, no. But her heart declares, "Because of God's love, *I am* clean, innocent, pure, loved, adored and accepted by the One who matters most in a fallen world."

The Shulamite woman is *His love* among the daughters. You are God's loved one among everyone else. Your heart stands out among those around you. You may say, "That can't be true; you don't know my heart." God knows, and He loves you. If as you read this, there is something that is tugging at your heart that you need to repent of, then do that—repent.

Your uniqueness is very precious to the Lord; always remember that. That's why there is never a need for you to try to be something or someone that you are not. Just be who God created you to be, and live loved.

"A Christian is not simply a person who is forgiven and goes to heaven. A Christian, in terms of his or her deepest identity, is a saint, a spiritually born child of God, a divine masterpiece, a child of light, a citizen of heaven." Neil T. Anderson

Embrace your uniqueness, and quit running from it. When you are standing in a room full of people, you are the most loved and adored person by God in that room. And He feels the same about everyone else in the room! That's the depth of His love! He loves each of His sons and daughters with the same intensity, making each person feel as if they are the most special person in all the world to Him. That's love.

I feel that there is someone reading this that has felt they had to suppress their creative and unique heart because of being rejected by others in the past. Just know that Father God has not rejected you; He loves your heart. He loves how He made you so unique.

Right now, I break off of you the spirit of rejection, and I pray that you are filled to overflowing with Father's great love so that you can be who God created you to be.

"For we are His workmanship, created in Christ Jesus for good works, which God prepared beforehand that we should walk in them." Ephesians 2:10

PERSONAL APPLICATION

You are unique before God. There is no one else like you in the world. As you are learning through this book, beauty and worth are how God defines your heart, not what you look like on the outside. We all come in many different shapes and sizes, and that's just the way it is. This may seem a little silly to you, but I challenge you to give this a try: Find a mirror in your home, and give yourself a good long look. What do you see? What do you feel? That person staring across from you is God's beloved! That person staring across from you has a beautiful and wonderful heart. When you really get this revelation, you can look in the mirror and literally feel a joy well up within you as you stare at the one who Jesus loves. If this is difficult to do, perhaps there is an area in your heart such as rejection, low self-esteem, or pain that God wants to heal. In the space provided, write what God shows you through this exercise:

_____
_____
_____
_____
_____
_____
_____
_____
_____
_____
_____
_____

Living Loved

6

ENJOYING GOD

"Like an apple tree among the trees of the woods, so is my beloved among the sons. I sat down in his shade with great delight, and his fruit was sweet to my taste."
Song of Songs 2:3

This is one of my favorite verses in this chapter of the Song of Songs. I really enjoy reading and meditating on this verse. This verse speaks of the refreshing, joyful and peaceful relationship that the love of God brings into our lives. It represents spiritual rest and enjoyment with a loving Father. Don't you just love the sound of that?

We need the revelation that we can enjoy God, anytime and anywhere. God is not just found in church gatherings, Bible studies, worship sets and prayer meetings. We can learn to "sit down in His shade" and enjoy Him in any place.

When I used to build houses many years ago, the construction workers would have their rock music blaring loud all day long. I usually could tune it out, but sometimes it would get to me. That's when I would find a place on the construction site where I could get alone with God, even if it was just for a few minutes, and "sit under His shade tree with great delight". And those moments would reset my heart. Friend, you can learn to enjoy God anywhere, because the kingdom of God is within you (this is the premise of my book, *Carrying The Presence: How To Bring The Kingdom Of God To Anyone, Anywhere*).

"...the kingdom of God is within you." Luke 17:21

And...

"...the kingdom of God is not eating and drinking, but righteousness and peace and joy in the Holy Spirit." Romans 14:17

If you have Jesus living inside you, then you can enjoy His presence anywhere. It's so good for you to learn to practice the presence of God as much as possible. Learn to lean back on Jesus within your heart, sit under the shade tree, and receive His love and enjoy His presence while you do even the most mundane of tasks in your life.

I share all the time on how our lives consist of thousands of ordinary moments—moments such as mowing the lawn, driving to work, taking a shower, cleaning the house, etc. It's in those thousands of ordinary moments that God wants you to learn to enjoy Him. God is just as enjoyable in the valley as He is on the mountaintop. If you understand what I am saying and put this into practice, many things in your life will begin to shift in the direction that God has planned for you. Many Christians live dissatisfied and disappointed in their walk with God, but He will always say to you, "I'm right here. Come away with Me. Come and sit with Me, and let Me love you and speak to your heart." You don't have to be disappointed in your walk with God. You can enjoy His presence on a regular basis if you can learn to sit for a moment, quiet yourself down, worship Him and just listen for His voice.

God wants you to come to Him daily so He can refresh your weary heart. The apple tree in this verse symbolizes the refreshing fruit among all of the other trees in the woods (the woods in the verse can speak of all humanity or the world we live in).

Imagine this: you are hiking through the woods for hours and hours, and you suddenly realize that you forgot to bring something to eat on the hike. Then all of a sudden, you stumble upon this beautiful apple tree, and the apples are ripe and ready to eat. You pick one of the apples from the tree, sit down in the shade and enjoy the refreshing fruit. That's what the Shulamite woman is saying here. Among everything else in the world (in the woods) to partake of, He is most enjoyable and refreshing—and nothing else compares. Nothing satisfies a believer's heart like spending time partaking of the goodness of God's love.

"The enjoyment of God is the only happiness with which our souls can be satisfied." Jonathan Edwards

There are many people that I know who were once very passionate about their relationship with Jesus, but because life took its toll on them for whatever reason, they have searched for enjoyment and pleasure in the things of this world rather than in God. In other words, they have replaced intimacy with God for the temporary satisfactions that the world gives. I am not saying these people are living in sin; they have just left their first Love. He is calling us all back to that beautiful and peaceful place of sitting under His shade tree.

For whatever reason, some people feel like God has let them down, so they find it difficult to come back to that intimate place of sweet communion. But the apple tree is still there, waiting—beckoning the return of His beloved sons and daughters. If that's you, today is your day to ask God to touch your heart and enjoy sweet fellowship once again.

Notice how she says in this verse, "I sat down…." Admittedly, this is one of the hardest things for me personally to do—sit and rest. Even though it is right and good to practice the Lord's presence throughout the day, we must also have times of sitting down and resting in His presence. For me, that time is in the early morning hours when everything is quiet. Jesus was a great example of this:

"Now in the morning, having risen a long while before daylight, He went out and departed to a solitary place; and there He prayed." Mark 1:35

We encounter Jesus in greater dimensions when we take the time to sit down and commune with Him. He loves those times with us. At the end of this book, I list many benefits and blessings that come from sitting at the feet of Jesus in the quiet place.

If there are not regular times in our lives where we sit down "in His shade", we are too busy. I have already taught you that we can encounter and enjoy God everywhere, yes. But we go deeper, and our hearts become more awakened, when we take the time to simply sit down with the Lord. Everyone has time to do this—EVERYONE. It boils down to priorities, choices, and decisions. It's not a good idea to tell God that you are too busy to spend quiet time with Him, because He will "help you" find time. How? By pointing out the many things in your life that are distractions and are unnecessary. I would rather make that decision on my own because I love Him.

You see, in resting, there is no striving. No laboring. No stress or anxiety. Just rest, love, and joyful fellowship. We grow in Him when we rest, not when we are striving and constantly stressed out. He wants us to sit in His shade—the atmosphere of being with Him.

When we would build houses in the summer months, it felt so good and refreshing to take a break, find a shady spot and drink something cold. I can remember leaning back in the shade and thoroughly enjoying even a ten minute break. That little moment was enough to reset and refresh the workers before they went back to work.

Throughout the day, take time to sit with the Lord and enjoy His presence, even if it's for just a few minutes. You will begin to see how effective this is for your life. He alone satisfies the weary soul.

One day, my brother and I were shoveling gravel for hours and hours. It was grueling work in the hot sun, and we were very thirsty. Unfortunately, all we had to drink was a few cans of diet soda. We each downed two sodas in the matter of a couple of minutes. Well, that didn't turn out too well for us. Both of us got immediately sick to our stomachs as we tried to go back to work. What we needed was water or Gatorade to refresh us, not diet soda! The soda did not quench our deep thirst. Nothing can quench a thirsty soul like the presence of God.

When you have an opportunity to take a break or two throughout the day with the Lord, just love Him, and let Him love you. That's all you need. You can open up your Bible, turn to a particular verse, thank the Lord for it, and meditate on His promises as He refreshes your soul. Or just take a few minutes and worship the Lord, and you will be refreshed. This is sitting under the shade tree, and you can do this every day. It's the secret place of God that we can all enter into when we make the Lord our dwelling place.

"He who dwells in the secret place of the Most High shall abide under the shadow of the Almighty." Psalm 91:1

The woman in our story sits under the shade tree with *great delight*. I love that. She is expressing how much spiritual pleasure is found in resting in the presence of the Lord. Again, sitting with the Lord throughout the day refreshes us, fills us up and rejuvenates our weary hearts. As you learn to practice the presence of the Lord, you will find your heart longing for the times under the shade tree more and more, because you realize not only how much you need Him, but the great delight that is found in being with Him.

"Oh, taste and see that the LORD is good; blessed is the man who trusts in Him!" Psalm 34:8

And this is what the Shulamite woman did in our story. She tasted the fruit of the tree. The fruit here can represent any fruit of the Spirit that you need.

"But the fruit of the Spirit is love, joy, peace, longsuffering, kindness, goodness, faithfulness, gentleness, self-control..." Galatians 5:22-23

What fruit do you need? Love? Joy? Peace? Find yourself a quiet place with God under the shade tree, and eat of the fruit that has been provided for you. Beloved, it's not enough to admire the fruit; we have to eat of it. How do you "eat" of this fruit? By meditating on the truths found in the Word of God regarding peace, joy, love, or anything else you need. Read a particular Scripture regarding your need, meditate on what the Holy Spirit is speaking to you, and then believe it, receive it, thank God for it and worship Him. Let His truths become part of your innermost being as you digest it into your spirit.

This precious young lady is beginning to learn *how to enjoy God and be enjoyed by God.* This is one of the greatest secrets of life: when we learn to *enjoy God,* it changes our entire outlook on life, and then when we learn how much *we are enjoyed by God,* we are never the same again. Beloved, you are enjoyed by God! What a profound thought that the Creator of the universe enjoys being with you! Here's more proof:

"The Lord your God in your midst, the Mighty One, will save; He will rejoice over you with gladness, He will quiet you with His love, He will rejoice over you with singing." Zephaniah 3:17

Friends, God really, really, really loves you! The Hebrew words in this Scripture reveal a God that has a glad and joyful heart over you, loves spending time with you, is dancing over you, is singing over you and is continually demonstrating His love for you. When we experience God's enjoyment of us, it awakens something deep within us, and we begin to live loved. When people ask me how I am doing today, many times I say, "Living loved!", because it's true! His love has filled my heart to overflowing. If God can love, adore and enjoy someone like me, He can do the same for you. I pray that while you have been reading this, His love has been breaking through to you.

You see, when your identity is in the right place, seeing yourself as a fragrant rose, a pure lily, and a son or daughter that is loved and cherished by God, you are a better receiver under the shade tree of His delight.

We will never enjoy the Lord's presence more than we have a revelation of the Lord enjoying us, even in our weakness. We don't want to continually come before His presence wrestling with the thoughts of, "What mood is God in today? Will He love me? Will He receive me?" Hearts that wrestle with wondering if they are loved by God will be easily disappointed when they don't actually feel loved at the moment. We can only clench our teeth and obey and seek God for so long before we quit obeying and searching for Him, unless we learn how to *enjoy God and be enjoyed by God in the midst of our walk with Him.* If we love Him, we will obey Him and continually seek His heart.

"He who has My commandments and keeps them, it is he who loves Me. And he who loves Me will be loved by My Father, and I will love him and manifest Myself to him." John 14:21

Our obedience *to* God flows out of our love *for* God. And when you are truly in love with someone, you are willing to do anything for that person. In regard to obedience, some believers look at the Bible as being restrictive, but it's protective—it's love. If you feel as if Christianity is restrictive, then you don't know Jesus very well. Again, we obey Him because we love Him so deeply. There is no sacrifice too great for someone that is in love.

"To love God is the greatest of virtues; to be loved by God is the greatest of blessings." Author Unknown

PERSONAL APPLICATION

It's time to sit under the shade tree with great delight. Today, find yourself a quiet place where you know that you will not be disturbed. Just get quiet before God, and meditate on His love for you. Think about those things you have already gleaned from this book. Tell God how much you love Him and want to live in His presence all the time. Don't write down anything yet. Just spend quality time, loving God and being loved by God. Let His love, joy and peace refresh you as you partake of this fruit. Now, after a time of sitting with the Lord, write down those things that you felt or heard God whisper to your heart:

_____
_____
_____
_____
_____
_____
_____
_____
_____
_____
_____
_____
_____
_____
_____
_____
_____

Living Loved

7

THE BANQUETING HOUSE

"He brought me to the banqueting house, and his banner over me was love." Song of Songs 2:4

You have been invited to the banqueting house of God. In fact, Jesus actually brought you there. He may have even carried you to the banqueting house. He's a good Father. He has brought us to the banqueting house (or house of wine) because He loves us. He has brought His sons and daughters to the celebration of love and sweet communion. You and I are welcome at the Lord's table of love. He has prepared a feast of love and fellowship to spend time with each one us. All of His sons and daughters are invited; no one is left out. He brought you in because He loves you. It's not about deserving to be at the banqueting house; it's all because of His love for us.

It's at this banquet that He shares with us, from His heart, all the good and wonderful things that He has prepared for us. Everything you need and everything you are searching for in Him is found at the banquet. No matter what you have been through, what you have done or what your present situation looks like, you are welcomed into His house of love because you are His beloved.

In the banqueting house, there is only One that matters—Jesus. All of us are sitting together fellowshipping, but we are there for Him.

"We love Him because He first loved us." 1 John 4:19

Thank you, Jesus, for bringing us into the banqueting house so that we can enjoy sweet fellowship together with our brothers and sisters. The ultimate banquet will be on that great day when we are all sitting together at the marriage supper of the Lamb (see Revelation 17:9).

BANNER OF LOVE

His love *for* us is His banner *over* us. It's *His* banner that's over me—His banner of love. It's a banner of love that has proven that He has captured our hearts and conquered the enemy by paying the highest price of giving His life for us. As this banner waves over us, He is declaring that we are His loved ones.

Friend, the banner over your life is love—not shame, condemnation, pain, rejection, sorrow and the like. Your identity and how you think and feel about yourself must be in agreement with what God has declared over you—the banner of love. He defines my life by His love for me. I know what things in my life need to change. God knows what things in my life need to change. But His banner over me is still love.

NO MORE SHAME

Let's talk about shame for a moment. Have you ever heard someone say, "Shame on you!"? Maybe someone has said it to you. There is someone that is continually trying to say that to you—public enemy #1—Satan himself, the accuser. He whispers in the ears of Christians on a regular basis, "Shame on you."

You see, guilt says, "I did something wrong; I need to repent and change." Shame says, "There is something wrong with me as a person." Condemnation takes it to the next level and says, "I am no good. Something is wrong with me. I am not loved by God. I am worthless. Etc." Condemnation can leave someone with a feeling of utter despair and hopelessness.

What does shame sound like in someone's life? Here are some examples of the voice of shame: "Everyone thinks you are a good mother—you're not. You're a fake. You are always yelling at your kids; you are always stressed out; you never have time for your kids; your kids don't listen to you. Look at yourself; you're a failure as a mom." Or, "You have to work two jobs, Dad, because you are not a good provider; you can't hold down a job; you're a failure as a father and as a husband. Everyone thinks you're weak; you should be walking with your head down." Or, "You're ugly and overweight; what's wrong with you? Nobody loves you." Or, "You are never good at anything." Or, "You have sinned too much; God only tolerates you; He doesn't even love you." Or, "You will never get out of debt; you are horrible with money. Shame on you." And the list goes on.

You see, when we have shame, it weighs us down. It weighs down our hearts, our emotions, our prayer life, our relationships, etc. Shame tries to steal our confidence in the truth that we are loved by God. Some have walked in shame for decades because of what they have done in the past—something that God has long ago forgiven them of. We may think that because we are surprised by our sin and weaknesses, somehow God is too. Let me tell you something: NOTHING you say or do takes God by surprise, ever.

So how do we deal with shame? Basically, shame enters a heart that does not understand God's heart. When we lack confidence in God and what He really feels and thinks about us in all situations, it can open the door to bring in shame.

"No child of God sins to the degree as to make himself incapable of forgiveness." John Bunyan

But let me tell you, you are amazing to God. Others may not think so. Others may misunderstand you. Others may try to hurt and wound you or make fun of you. But your Father in Heaven thinks you're beautiful and wonderful, inside and out!

Rebuke all shame that tries to come near you, and guard against it in the future by the revelation of what your Father thinks and feels about you. You didn't get the job promotion—it's ok. There is something better around the corner, because Father says so. You haven't met someone to marry yet, but instead of shame, you see that Father's timing is perfect, and it's not you. It's all about His timing. You don't make friends well—instead of embracing shame, draw close to God and know that there is no friend as close as Jesus. Someone doesn't like your singing voice—it's ok! Heaven stops to listen every time you sing, because you are touching God's heart.

We are the ones that give shame permission to come in and set up shop in our hearts. You may not feel very beautiful or handsome, so shame tries to come, but instead, take a deep breath, quiet yourself, and hear the Father whisper to your heart, "I love you. You are so beautiful. You take my breath away when I look at you. I created you, and therefore, you are perfect. I NEVER create a mess or make a mistake. I create beauty. Beauty is in the eye of the beholder, and I am the One beholding you. You are loved!"

Shame also tries to come in because of our sin. Everyone sins. Everyone. Repentance is obviously priority number one when we do sin. We know that. Without repentance, we can't be forgiven. Without repentance, we won't feel clean (Read Psalm 51), pure, or confident in God. When we sin, it tries to rob us of our confidence in God. And if we don't understand God's heart, when we sin, it can lead to years of tremendous, debilitating shame.

If you sinned today in word, thought or deed, repent and move on. Why? Because if you don't, shame will want to come in. His Blood is enough. Period! When you ask Jesus to forgive you and wash you clean, in His eyes, it never even happened. But shame says, "No one can love you that much. No one can forgive so quickly." But Jesus does—every time. The moment you asked for forgiveness from your heart, His Blood washed you clean.

"If we confess our sins, He is faithful and just to forgive us our sins and to cleanse us from all unrighteousness." 1 John 1:9

"But you don't know what I have done!" Friend, you have to realize what Jesus did! He didn't just pay for some sins, He paid for all our sins. Not only is He faithful to forgive us, but to cleanse us also. There is nothing like a clean heart. Quit putting yourself on "spiritual probation" because of what you have done. We don't crawl back to God hoping He will maybe, perhaps have a little love left over for us. No.

If you have done something in your past that you are very ashamed of, here's what you do: first, ask God to forgive you. Then, you may have to ask others to forgive you. It may be something that you need to tell someone, maybe not. The important thing is that your heart is right with God. Ask Him to forgive you for all the years you have beat yourself up and allowed shame to have a place in your heart. You are clean now. Don't go back to those thoughts again. Command all shame to go, feel the shackles fall off of you, and live in your freedom.

If you deal with habitual sin and live in constant shame, remember that He has given you the power to overcome. You can be set free from habitual sin, right now. As you know, habitual sin is very destructive—not only because it affects our lives (and the lives of others), but also because it affects our relationship with the Lord. It's a nasty cycle within a person where the enemy will make you feel like there is no hope and that you will never be free. We don't have to believe that lie, because through Christ, we can always overcome, as He has given us the grace and power to do so. And the more we are rooted and grounded in the Father's love, the stronger our resolve will be to only live in such a way that pleases Him in everything we think or do.

If you are dealing with habitual sin, repent for the sin, command shame to loose you and let you go, and declare victory over the area that once held you bound. You are now free. No more shackles. And the shame is gone. You are a new person. It's a new day. Renew your mind with the Word of God (see chapter 19) where there was once a stronghold of sin. What once had you bound in shame is now your testimony and one of your greatest victories.

And remember, the foundation of our hearts must be built on what God thinks and feels about us. Otherwise, it will bring shame. DO NOT listen to shame any longer; listen to love—God's perfect, beautiful, everlasting love.

"Love has reasons which reason cannot understand" Blaise Pascal

HIS BANNER IS ALWAYS LOVE

Right now, dear one, you have a banner of love waving over you. The enemy also knows that this banner of love is waving over you, so he does what he can to come between you and Father's love for you. However, if you continue to learn to live in God's presence, keeping your heart pure before Him and living loved, the enemy will have no foothold in your life. The devil hates love. He hates the Father, and he hates you. When you live loved, it drives him crazy!

Any area in our lives that doesn't come under the banner of love runs the risk of being religious. Love must flow in, and love must flow out.

When we stumble, His banner over us is love. When we have a bad day, His banner over us is love. When people misunderstand us or mistreat us, His banner over us is love. When our finances are not doing well, His banner over us is love. When we are sick, His banner over us is love. When our marriages are at a low point, His banner over us is love. When we can't seem to feel or hear the Lord, His banner over us is love. When our circumstances in life seem out of control, His banner over us is love. So, no matter what we are facing in our lives, the banner over us is His love. Embrace it. Rest in it. Believe it. Walk in it. And live out of His love.

OVERRULED

From now on, when any negative emotion or lie from the enemy tries to attack you, tell those things that they have been OVERRULED by Father's love! When the enemy brings up your past, say, "OVERRULED by Father's love." When people mistreat you, stand firm, and say, "OVERRULED by Father's loving embrace." His love overrules the pain, shame, regret, and even the bad memories of the past. Just receive His love now.

Why don't you start living like you are forgiven? Whatever you don't feel forgiven of will continue to try to replay in your mind. His love and His blood have covered you.

Always remember that Jesus is the same yesterday, today and forever (see Hebrews 13:8), so His love for you is the same yesterday, today and forever.

"God has cast our confessed sins into the depths of the sea, and He's even put a 'No Fishing' sign over the spot." D. L. Moody

PERSONAL APPLICATION

Is there any area in your life where you have not forgiven yourself, even though you have asked God to forgive you? Do you still battle shame and condemnation? The enemy loves to remind us of all our wrongdoing to keep us from living loved. Today, ask the Lord to set you free from shame and condemnation as you pour out your heart before Him. Meditate on these powerful verses:

"Bless the Lord, O my soul; and all that is within me, bless His holy name! Bless the Lord, O my soul, and forget not all His benefits: Who forgives all your iniquities, who heals all your diseases, who redeems your life from destruction, who crowns you with lovingkindness and tender mercies, who satisfies your mouth with good things, so that your youth is renewed like the eagle's. The Lord executes righteousness and justice for all who are oppressed. He made known His ways to Moses, His acts to the children of Israel. The Lord is merciful and gracious, slow to anger, and abounding in mercy. He will not always strive with us, nor will He keep His anger forever. He has not dealt with us according to our sins, nor punished us according to our iniquities. For as the heavens are high above the earth, so great is His mercy toward those who fear Him; as far as the east is from the west, so far has He removed our transgressions from us. As a father pities his children, so the Lord pities those who fear Him. For He knows our frame; He remembers that we are dust." Psalm 103:1-14

What is the Lord revealing to you through this powerful Scripture? Write those things here:

_____
_____
_____
_____
_____
_____
_____
_____
_____
_____
_____
_____
_____
_____
_____
_____
_____
_____
_____
_____
_____
_____
_____
_____
_____
_____
_____
_____

8

LOVESICK

"Sustain me with cakes of raisins, refresh me with apples, for I am lovesick." Song of Songs 2:5

This should be the desire of each one of our hearts: to be lovesick for Jesus. To be lovesick for Jesus means that from the depths of our being, we long to know and love Him more than anything else in this life. We long to spend time with Him every moment that we can. To be lovesick is to hunger and thirst (see Matthew 5:6) continually for Him. Here's how King David described it:

"O God, You are my God; early will I seek You; my soul thirsts for You; my flesh longs for You in a dry and thirsty land where there is no water. So I have looked for You in the sanctuary, to see Your power and Your glory. Because Your lovingkindness is better than life, my lips shall praise You. Thus I will bless You while I live; I will lift up my hands in Your name." Psalm 63:1-4

BETTER THAN WINE

To be lovesick is to desire Jesus more than anything else this world has to offer. In Song of Songs 1:2, the Shulamite woman announces:

"Let him kiss me with the kisses of his mouth—for your love is better than wine."

Better than wine...what does that mean to us? Those who are in love with Jesus understand that His intimate (kisses) love is "better than" any pleasures this world has to offer. The momentary pleasures of this world will never satisfy the longing within us to encounter the love of God. These worldly pleasures are inferior to all that we can experience in God. To be lovesick is to desire and pursue God's love, presence, joy, fellowship, etc. more than anything else in life. To be lovesick is to live in the revelation of the beauty and power of God. To be lovesick is to desire Him morning, noon, night, and midnight snack!

You see, the subtle deception is that the things of this world do temporarily satisfy our souls, but not our spirits. Our souls crave worldly pleasures. Our spirits crave the pleasures of God. This is why we have to be careful with what we are yielding ourselves to in this world. Obviously, not all pleasure we experience as humans is wrong, as it's a very important part of how God created us. However, what I am saying is that there is absolutely no substitute, or any greater or lasting pleasure, in anything this world has to offer compared to the eternal pleasures of intimately knowing God. This verse encapsulates the heart of what I am saying:

"They are abundantly satisfied with the fullness of Your house, and You give them drink from the river of Your pleasures." Psalm 36:8

Beloved, we should long to be lovesick for Jesus.

Jesus was once asked what the greatest commandment is. Here's what He said:

"...You shall love the LORD your God with all your heart, with all your soul, with all your strength, and with all your mind..." Luke 10:27

Father wants us to love Him with our all, because He loves us with His all. Jesus wants us to love Him the way that He loves us.

Father's first priority for us is that we would cultivate love for Jesus every single day—drawing closer to His heart, hearing His voice and falling deeper and deeper in love with Him, while at the same time loosening our grip from all those things that are holding us back.

We learn to love God by understanding His love for us. God has everything, yet He is searching for something that He still needs. What does God search for? What does He want first and foremost? Our love. It is love that He is after. He is after our hearts. The mystery of the Christian life is found in this truth!

LOVING WITH ALL OF YOUR HEART

To be lovesick is to love Jesus with all of your heart. By loving Jesus with all of your heart, you are able to love God on an emotional level—on a heart level. Love is more than what we simply say to God with our lips. Love is how our hearts feel and respond to God in love.

"For where your treasure is, there your heart will be also." Matthew 6:21

What your heart treasures, values, and is lovesick for, there your heart will be also. Do you want to know what you treasure and value more than anything else in your life? Do you want to know what your heart is lovesick for? Here's a pop quiz:

What do you spend the most time on in your life?

What do you love the most in your life?

What do you spend your money on?

What are you always thinking about?

What is your heart's desire?

Again, whatever it is in your life that you are placing the most value, time, money, and affection on, that's where you will find your heart. Think about it for a while. Are you lovesick for Him? To be lovesick for Jesus is an essential part of living loved. Our relationships with Jesus should continually be, "I love Jesus, and Jesus loves me!"

"I am my beloved's, and my beloved is mine..." Song of Songs 6:3

Our emotional makeup is an essential part of how God created us. He created our hearts with a great capacity to love and to be loved. The more that we yield our hearts to God, the more we can encounter His love, the more we will live loved, the more we will love Him in return and the more we will love others.

We love others to the degree that we ourselves feel loved by God. Please don't ever forget that. The more you live loved, the more your heart will be bursting with love for those around you. If you struggle with loving others, I'm sure that you struggle with loving yourself.

"Keep your heart with all diligence, for out of it spring the issues of life." Proverbs 4:23

Daily, we have to keep a watch on our hearts to stay pure and clean before Him so we don't hinder the flow of love. Christianity is an ongoing encounter of love with a Person, not a religion. Our hearts were designed to long for love, and this love is experienced to its depth and height and width and breadth when it is experienced in the love of Jesus.

We can express our love to God every day as we draw nearer and nearer to His heart. Our love for God originates from our hearts, not from our heads. Love flows from my heart to His heart and then back to my heart, and that's how we encounter His love. That's how we live loved!

'I am Thine, O Lord, I have heard Thy voice,
And it told Thy love to me;
But I long to rise in the arms of faith
And be closer drawn to Thee.

Draw me nearer, nearer blessed Lord,
To the cross where Thou hast died;
Draw me nearer, nearer, nearer blessed Lord,
To Thy precious, bleeding side.

Consecrate me now to Thy service, Lord,
By the pow'r of grace divine;
Let my soul look up with a steadfast hope,
And my will be lost in Thine.

Oh, the pure delight of a single hour
That before Thy throne I spend,
When I kneel in prayer, and with Thee, my God
I commune as friend with friend!

There are depths of love that I cannot know
Till I cross the narrow sea;
There are heights of joy that I may not reach
Till I rest in peace with Thee."

Draw Me Nearer, Frances Crosby

LOVING WITH ALL OF YOUR MIND

To be lovesick with your mind is to continually fill your mind with thoughts that draw you closer to Jesus and not those thoughts that draw you away from Him.

"And do not be conformed to this world, but be transformed by the renewing of your mind, that you may prove what is that good and acceptable and perfect will of God." Romans 12:2

The thoughts that we think greatly affect how we respond to Jesus in love. Friend, the truth is, when you are lovesick, you don't have to force your mind to think about Jesus. When you are in love with someone, you don't have to try to "work something up" or force yourself to think about that person, right? The fact is, you can't stop thinking about them all day! When our minds are renewed through the truths of the Word of God, He will continually be in our thoughts. If we are continually filling our minds with the junk of this world, how can we remain lovesick for Jesus?

"Finally, brethren, whatever things are true, whatever things are noble, whatever things are just, whatever things are pure, whatever things are lovely, whatever things are of good report, if there is any virtue and if there is anything praiseworthy—meditate on these things." Philippians 4:8

Our minds are the entryway to how our hearts respond to the Lord in love. Much of the way we live begins in the mind. We are not always able to resist all thoughts that come into our mind, but we can redirect them according to what we read in Philippians 4:8. We love Jesus with all of our mind by reading and meditating on God's Word on a regular basis and keeping our minds continually directed toward Heaven.

"If then you were raised with Christ, seek those things which are above, where Christ is, sitting at the right hand of God. Set your mind on things above, not on things on the earth." Colossians 3:1-2

What do you fill your mind with? When you are lovesick, your thoughts are continually on Jesus.

"Real prayer is communion with God, so that there will be common thoughts between His mind and ours. What is needed is for Him to fill our hearts with His thoughts, and then His desires will become our desires flowing back to Him." A.W. Pink

LOVING WITH ALL OF YOUR STRENGTH

To be lovesick with all of your strength is to give the Lord the best part of your day. Jesus does not want or deserve our "leftovers"; He wants to be with us when we are at our best. Sometimes we tend to only seek God when we are worn out or desperate. It's fine to do that, of course, but He also wants to be with us when we are doing great in life. This is a sacrifice; this is a choice that we each make. But I feel it's deeper than simply making a choice to be with Him. When we are lovesick, we desire to spend time with Him at any hour, no matter how we are doing spiritually, physically, or emotionally.

"Every Christian would agree that a man's spiritual health is exactly proportional to his love for God." C. S. Lewis

We also can love the Lord with our strength by being His hands and feet extended to the world around us. We demonstrate our love for God by reaching out to the hurting and broken in this world. It's really no effort or sacrifice to touch the world around us when we are lovesick for Jesus. The lovesick will do anything and go anywhere for the One they love.

"I believe that Jesus would have given His life for just one person. Jesus emptied Himself, He humbled Himself and He so yielded Himself to His Father's love that He had no ambition of His own. He was not looking to build an empire, He did not want praise or adulation or to impress people with

who or how many followed Him. He stopped over and over again for just one person, for just one life." Heidi Baker

LOVING WITH ALL OF YOUR SOUL

To be lovesick with all of your soul is to love Jesus with the very core of who you are—even those places that are "untouchable" to everyone else, those hidden and hallowed places within each one of us. Those who are lovesick have yielded even the deepest places within them over to Jesus. Our soul must be healed and yielded to Jesus if we are to mature in our love for Him.

This is not always easy to do, because our soulish makeup is interwoven with many things that have happened to us or even been passed down to us through previous generations. However, when we pursue the heart of God, He will bring those deep and tender places to light so they can be healed and replaced with His great love.

This is the area where many Christians are held back from being lovesick. They feel a roadblock, a hindrance, or some sort of wall up within their heart that keeps them from knowing and receiving the depths of God's love. When we take care of deep issues, it will release our souls in freedom to be lovesick like a bird being released from a cage. It will be difficult for you to love God and receive His love if your soul is entangled with many issues. God longs for His children to be healed deep within their soul.

Again, many believers are held back by a wounded and offended soul because of the past. They feel like they have been through too much in life to be able to fully surrender their soul to God. But that's what the enemy wants you to think. Yes, you may have been through very severe and traumatic things in your life that have affected you deeply, but there is no place within a person's heart where God's love cannot reach.

To love Jesus with all of our soul is to bring Him all the pain, all the shame, all the trauma, all the woundedness, all the regret, all the hurt, all the fear and all the anger and ask Him to heal us and replace those things with His love.

"How do I know if there are areas that have not been yielded or healed in my soul?" Ask Jesus. He will show you what is hindering the flow of love in those deep places. For instance, if you battle low self-esteem, ask the Lord to show you how that came into your life, seek His healing power in that place, and ask Him to fill that void with His love. Once you have a revelation of a place in your soul that needs to be yielded and healed, take care of business with God, and receive His love in that area. You would be amazed at how many soulish issues are hindering our love walk with God.

"Troubled soul, the 'much tribulation' will soon be over, and as you enter the 'kingdom of God' you shall then see, no longer 'through a glass darkly' but in the unshadowed sunlight of the Divine presence, that 'all things' did 'work together' for your personal and eternal good." A. W. Pink

SEEKING AND FINDING

It's much easier to love the Lord when you are lovesick, as opposed to feeling condemned for not seeking Him with all of your heart, mind, soul and strength. How do you become lovesick? By daily seeking to know Him through abiding in His presence.

I'm afraid that most Christians are not seeking the Lord with all of their hearts, because they are not really sure what they are searching for.

"And you will seek Me and find Me, when you search for Me with all your heart." Jeremiah 29:13

Let's say that I came over to your home, sat your family down and told you that somewhere in your house, I hid a brand new, crisp $1 bill. This $1 bill could be hidden in the attic, under the floorboards, buried in the wall, embedded in the plumbing—it could be anywhere. Then I told you to seek out this $1 bill, and when you found it, it would be yours. Then I told you to go for it! What would your response be? You would probably say, "Thanks, but no thanks. I think we'll pass on that offer. We are not going to tear our house apart for one measly dollar." Why? Because searching for $1 is not worth all the trouble and effort it would take to find it.

Now let's take that same scenario, and instead of me telling you that there is a $1 bill hidden in your house, I tell you that it's a check made out to your family in the amount of 10 million dollars. Again, it could be hidden anywhere. How would you respond? You would, of course, work day and night, 24/7 until you found that check. Why? Because of the incredible value of what you would find. You would seek that 10 million dollars with all of your heart, because you know what would happen when you found it.

It's the same with seeking the Lord with all of our heart. If we don't think He's a good Father, or if we think nothing will ever happen when we pray, that we are somehow the "black sheep" of God's family or that God doesn't love us, we will not go on searching for God with all of our heart, mind, soul and strength. And when we don't seek Him, we don't find Him. It's that simple.

If you would simply understand the great reward that comes to us when we search for God with all of our heart, it would make any level of seeking Him entirely worth it.

"Finding God" is the greatest experience a person could ever have while on this earth. There is no close second. There is no price too great to pay to be close and stay close to Jesus. He is everything we need, desire and are looking for in this life.

LIVING LOVESICK

Beloved, those who are lovesick for Jesus can make it through anything. I have seen many Christians lose their heart, faith and love for God in recent years because they did not remain in love with Jesus. You see, one of the wonderful blessings of living in love with Jesus is that He takes you from glory to glory (see 2 Corinthians 3:18). When we remain passionately in love with Jesus, He causes all things to work together for our good (see Romans 8:28)—even the bad things that have happened to us. If things are not good in your life yet, then God isn't done working! We don't give up, give in, yield to a sinful lifestyle or backslide when we are lovesick.

We have to cultivate our love for God every day. This world and the god of this world will continually try to pull us out of passionate love for God. To keep passion for Jesus burning hot within you is not difficult to do. It's the basics of Christianity. Stay in His Word, pray, worship, pray in tongues as much as possible, keep your heart pure, etc. You already know what to do, but it's amazing how easily distracted we can get, even from the basics. Personally, I am asking Jesus to give me the grace to live lovesick for Him to the point where I feel as if I can't ever get enough of Him. We will never, ever exhaust the supply of all the good things that God has for us as we seek Him with all of our hearts.

Picture this: I build a huge, roaring bonfire in the middle of an open field on a cold, dark, winter night. You are standing two hundred yards away from the bonfire. I am yelling for you to come closer to the fire, but you can't hear me—you're too far away; you're just standing there. I call you on your cellphone, and you immediately tell me that you're cold and that you can't feel the fire. Confused, I tell you to come closer, and you will encounter the fire. You take a few steps and then stop again, and I'm thinking, "What is going on with this person? They are cold, and it's dark way out there, yet they are not running toward the fire, and they are acting like it's too far to walk."

Being lovesick for Jesus in this dark and cold world is to move closer and closer to the bonfire of His fiery heart. And the closer we get to His heart, the more we encounter Him in ways we have always longed for. Unfortunately, many Christians are standing too far away from Jesus to encounter Him. But I believe there is going to be a fresh, global awakening of the Father's love for us—an awakening that will impact the entire Body of Christ. Can you imagine multitudes of believers living in the love of the Father? It will cause our love for each other to rise to a whole new level.

Beloved, come closer to the fire. Come closer to His fiery and passionate heart for you. Come closer, and feel the warmth of His love. Let His fire touch every part of your heart.

"May God so fill us today with the heart of Christ that we may glow with the divine fire of holy desire." A.B. Simpson

Ask the Lord to sustain your heart with more of Him ("cakes of raisins"). Pray that He satisfies your heart with the good things of His kingdom. There is plenty available for you right now, no matter what is going on in your life.

"Oh, taste and see that the LORD is good; blessed is the man who trusts in Him!" Psalm 34:8

Then ask the Lord to refresh you with His joy and love ("with apples"). There is absolutely nothing in this world that can refresh and satisfy like Jesus can. You name it—at the end of the day, it all falls short of what only Jesus can give us.

I have had the privilege of being taken to Heaven several times. One of the things that stands out to me in those visits is the actual atmosphere of Heaven. The very atmosphere of Heaven is saturated with love, joy, and peace in 100% fullness. The feeling is so euphoric that earthly words cannot describe what it is like. I am telling you this because Jesus said to pray:

"Your kingdom come. Your will be done on earth as it is in Heaven." Matthew 6:10

Jesus literally gave us permission to invite Heaven to earth so that we can experience those things that Heaven has to offer right now. You can sit under the shade tree, enjoy the fruit of the Spirit and encounter the atmosphere of Heaven in your life. It will make you lovesick for more and more of Him. The more you eat of His fruit, the more you long for Him! Don't get too busy to sit and rest daily in His presence.

"O, let the place of secret prayer become to me the most beloved spot on earth." Andrew Murray

PERSONAL APPLICATION

I know that you desire to be lovesick for Jesus. I know that you desire to love Him with all of your heart, mind, soul, and strength. You know yourself better than anyone else, so in the space provided, write out the ways that you can personally begin to yield yourself to God in the four areas of loving Him.

Your heart:

_____
_____
_____
_____
_____
_____
_____
_____
_____
_____

Your mind:

_____
_____
_____
_____
_____
_____
_____

Your soul:

Your strength:

9

THE HANDS OF FATHER

"His left hand is under my head, and his right hand embraces me." Song of Songs 2:6

As any good and loving father would, Father God loves to embrace His children. How does a God that we cannot see embrace us? He embraces us with His love, joy, peace, presence, blessings, etc. Even though we are not motivated in our walk with God by what we feel or don't feel (everything requires faith), when it comes to the embrace of Father God, He does often tangibly visit us. We *can* feel His presence. We *can* feel His love. We *can* feel His joy. Father God also has these same emotions, and when He visits us, we can feel what He feels.

There is nothing that can compare to receiving a touch from God. Personally, I am asking God for more of His tangible presence on a regular basis. Again, we don't measure our love walk with God based on how we feel at the moment; we trust His unfailing Word. If He says He loves us, then that's all we need to know, because His Word is truth and does not change.

In our story, the Shulamite woman is feeling the embrace of the one she loves. She feels so loved and protected by his hands.

"You have hedged me behind and before, and laid Your hand upon me." Psalm 139:5

Friend, God has laid His hands upon you to demonstrate His love for you.

We read in the opening verse that His left hand is under her head. That really touches me because it seems so tender. To you and me, the left hand represents the invisible movements of God. It's out of your view, because it's behind your head. It speaks of what Father is doing in your life that you cannot see. Don't you love that? This is an incredible hidden expression of His love for you. It's all those things that He is doing in your life that you cannot see or necessarily discern. It could be something that He is sparing you from like trouble, pain, or sorrow. He is doing more behind the scenes on our behalf than we realize. This is love.

"And when the servant of the man of God arose early and went out, there was an army, surrounding the city with horses and chariots. And his servant said to him, 'Alas, my master! What shall we do?' So he answered, 'Do not fear, for those who are with us are more than those who are with them.' And Elisha prayed, and said, 'Lord, I pray, open his eyes that he may see.' Then the Lord opened the eyes of the young man, and he saw. And behold, the mountain was full

of horses and chariots of fire all around Elisha." 2 Kings 6:15-17

This story from 2 Kings illustrates that God is moving on our behalf even though we don't always see or discern what He is doing. It's the invisible activity of God in our lives.

"It is in the deepest darkness of the starless midnight that men learn how to hold on to the hidden Hand most tightly and how that Hand holds them; that He sees where we do not, and knows the way He takes; and though the way be to us a roundabout way, it is the right way." A. T. Pierson

There are many things in the hidden movements of God that have been withheld from us that would have caused us great sorrow, pain, trauma or grief if He wasn't embracing us. There are even times when the Lord has nudged us in one direction versus another because of harm that would have come to us. This is love.

"If the Lord be with us, we have no cause of fear. His eye is upon us, His arm over us, His ear open to our prayer—His grace sufficient, His promise unchangeable." John Newton

Father's right hand is the one that embraces us. This speaks of the sweet, beautiful, tangible, manifest presence of God that can be seen, felt, and discerned. Beloved, when you feel the embrace of God, you become undone. Sometimes you weep. Sometimes you laugh with a heart full of joy. And sometimes you just sit in awe and wonder. But you feel Him.

He is there. He is so close. His presence is so evident. It's something that you never forget.

This embrace changes you. It enlarges your heart. It changes how you feel about yourself and others. It puts a new song in your heart and on your lips (see Psalm 40:3). It tenderizes even the hardest places in our hearts. It makes us broken, soft and pliable before God. It changes how you treat your brothers and sisters in the Lord. It changes your family. It affects how you work, play, and spend your time. This embrace fills voids and heals hearts. Nothing—and I mean nothing—on this earth compares to the embrace of Father.

"A believer longs after God: to come into His presence, to feel His love, to feel near to Him in secret, to feel in the crowd that he is nearer than all the creatures. Ah! dear brethren, have you ever tasted this blessedness? There is greater rest and solace to be found in the presence of God for one hour, than in an eternity of the presence of man." Robert Murray McCheyne

As believers, we are the extended hands of God to the world around us. Though everyone can experience Father's loving embrace for themselves, He uses Christians to bring His love to others through our own hands. I have literally prayed for hundreds of people, gently putting my hands on them, and they have wept and wept in front of me because they felt the love of the Father flowing into them in those precious moments. This obviously had nothing to do with me, but it was Father's love flowing through a willing vessel. He longs to flow through each one of us to reveal His love to others.

Several years ago, I was preaching in Pennsylvania to a large group of teenagers. About a week later, I received a beautiful email from one of the teenagers that I had prayed for who said that they had never felt love like that before. God's love overwhelmed this young person to the point where they said it changed everything they thought about God and now they truly knew that God loved them.

I was privileged to have been part of the Brownsville Revival (in Pensacola, Florida) in the 90's. We were actively involved in street outreach every Friday and Saturday night for years. We have many testimonies of people that were saved, healed and delivered during that time. We were the hands of Father God to these beautiful people. We prayed for so many people who God touched right on the spot, and they were forever changed—all because someone extended their hand to pray for them. This is so important for us as believers—to be the hands of Father God extended. When we extend our hands out to others to pray for them or even to greet them, it's as if Father God is reaching out Himself to touch them.

I pray for people everywhere I go, asking if I may place my hand on them as I pray, and most of the time, they feel the tangible presence of God, whether they actually know the Lord or not.

Beloved, the more that we live loved, the greater the flow of Father's love that will be released everywhere we go!

"Christ has no body but yours,
No hands, no feet on earth but yours,
Yours are the eyes with which He looks
Compassion on this world,
Yours are the feet with which he walks to do good,
Yours are the hands, with which He blesses all the world.
Yours are the hands, yours are the feet,
Yours are the eyes, you are His body.
Christ has no body now on earth but yours…"
Teresa of Avila

PERSONAL APPLICATION

In the space provided, write down a testimony of a time when you feel that Father God's hand was on your life to spare you from something terrible that *could have* happened. Then write down a time when you felt the tangible presence of God in your life:

_____
_____
_____
_____
_____
_____
_____
_____
_____
_____
_____
_____
_____
_____
_____
_____
_____
_____
_____
_____
_____
_____
_____
_____

Living Loved

10

PLEASE LEAVE ME ALONE

"I charge you, O daughters of Jerusalem, by the gazelles or by the does of the field, do not stir up nor awaken love until it pleases." Song of Songs 2:7

I don't know about you, but when I am spending time with the Lord, even the smallest of disruptions can feel so upsetting. In this verse, the Shulamite woman is basically saying to the daughters of Jerusalem, please leave me alone, as I am on a journey of love. My Beloved is doing something deep within my heart.

Gazelles and does tend to be very skittish, easily distracted, startled, and scared. So, she is asking the daughters to be patient with her. Please be gentle, loving, and understanding with what God is doing in my life. You know that feeling when God is taking you through a process. Sometimes you just need to be left alone as you are taking new steps in your journey toward the heart of God. You don't need to be judged or criticized, just left alone. Always remember that people criticize what they don't understand. This could be coming from someone in church, at work or even in your own home. No one can truly understand what is going on in the heart of someone else. If you want people to be patient and loving with you on your journey, please extend that same grace to others.

Don't expect people to always be happy for you or to be encouraging as you are on your journey with God. You have to do what God is telling you to do, no matter what everyone else thinks about it. And the sooner you make this decision, the better.

"For do I now persuade men, or God? Or do I seek to please men? For if I still pleased men, I would not be a bondservant of Christ." Galatians 1:10

You are responsible for your own heart before God. I want to encourage you to go after God's heart with all your heart, mind, soul, and strength, no matter what. Having this level of a pursuit of God's heart will open many doors *and* close many doors in your life. It will open doors of His love, presence, power, blessing, favor, divine appointments, etc. It will also close doors of wrong relationships, wrong opportunities, wasted time, etc.

Immature believers and those who are not actively pursuing God's heart cannot understand a heart that is in hot pursuit of God. No matter what, you keep your head up, and run, run, run after God like we see in the life of King David.

You are building your spiritual foundation by pursuing God's heart. You are developing your own history in God. You want to receive your own revelations from Him. You want to have your own encounters in His presence. There is nothing like encountering God for yourself. It's one thing to hear great teaching/preaching, but it's another thing for God to speak directly to your own heart.

There are books for you to write. There are songs for you to sing that the Lord gave you. There are ideas that God wants to impart to you. There are opportunities that He wants to reveal to you. There is so much creativity in you. You are destined for great things in your life as you spend time receiving from the Lord. Your best days are not behind you. If you would simply find the time on a regular basis to get alone with God, He would reveal Himself to you. He is not withholding His love from you. He is not withholding any good thing from you.

"For the LORD God is a sun and shield; the LORD will give grace and glory; no good thing will He withhold from those who walk uprightly." Psalm 84:11

I have had many well-meaning people through the years try to "help me" define what God was doing in me and around me. Some were right on in their prophetic word or wisdom, and others told me the very opposite of what God was whispering to my heart.

At the end of the day, nobody knows your heart like God does. He is always out for your best interest. He is always motivated by love in His plans for you. You can always trust and rely on Him. As you draw closer to Him, things will become clearer for you and your future. Tune out the noises and distractions around you, and set your gaze on Jesus. Those who spend much time with God change the world.

Investing your heart in being alone with God always works in your favor. Do you not think that God sees every movement of your heart toward Him? Do you not think that He longs to be with you and bless you exceedingly?

"Now to Him who is able to do exceedingly abundantly above all that we ask or think, according to the power that works in us..." Ephesians 3:20

Father is able to do more for you than you can even comprehend right now. Time alone with God is never wasted time. I have cried many, many tears and had great joy and peace in His presence. If God can come and visit me, He can visit you.

I feel that someone reading this is frustrated in hearing from God in the secret place of prayer. I want to submit that you *are* hearing Him. You just have to trust the still small voice within you. If you need to, write down what you feel He is communicating to your heart. This may help you to process what you feel God is saying to you.

There is no greater joy in this life than spending time alone with Jesus. There is also someone reading this who needs to be refreshed. I believe that when you go to the Lord in prayer, He will refresh your weary heart. Be sure to give Him all those things that have been heavy on your heart. You are loved!

"The discipline of time alone with God should not be looked at as another thing to put on your 'to do' list. This attitude will only lead to resentment from the added pressure that it produces. It should be viewed as a gift from a gracious and kind God. He cares so much for you and me that He is not just interested in our accomplishments but also in shepherding our hearts." William Thrasher

PERSONAL APPLICATION

As you read in the last chapter, time alone with God should be the highest priority in your life. Everything in your life should flow out of the secret place. I feel the longing in your heart increasing to spend more time with your Beloved. Sometimes you have to make certain decisions in your life to rearrange your priorities so you can be with Jesus. As you spend time with the Lord, write down what you feel He is saying to you in this season. Listen for His whisper, and lean into His love:

_____
_____
_____
_____
_____
_____
_____
_____
_____
_____
_____
_____
_____
_____
_____
_____
_____
_____
_____
_____

Living Loved

Living Loved

11

LEAPING AND SKIPPING

"The voice of my beloved! Behold, he comes leaping upon the mountains, skipping upon the hills." Song of Songs 2:8

Jesus is the One who has *already* conquered all that stands in the way of living loved!

The mountains in this Scripture represent the major natural or demonic barriers and strongholds that we come up against in life. It could be a major attack of some kind against our lives, our calling, our family, our future, etc. Whatever the mountain in your life may be, it has already been conquered. It has been conquered by the power and love of Jesus. He has leapt over that mountain you are facing.

"The mountains melt like wax at the presence of the Lord, at the presence of the Lord of the whole earth." Psalm 97:5

Listen for the voice of your Beloved, and He will give you revelation about the mountain you are facing. There is nothing that you are facing right now that He does not have the power to bring you through. Whatever you are going through will not change His love for you.

"Who shall separate us from the love of Christ? Shall tribulation, or distress, or persecution, or famine, or nakedness, or peril or sword? Yet in all these things we are more than conquerors through Him who loved us." Romans 8:35,37

We all come against mountain issues in our lives. Just know that the mountain has ALREADY been leapt over by Jesus because of His love for you. Now He's trying to win your heart over to implement the victory through you.

"So Jesus answered and said to them, 'Have faith in God. For assuredly, I say to you, whoever says to this mountain, "Be removed and be cast into the sea," and does not doubt in his heart, but believes that those things he says will be done, he will have whatever he says. Therefore I say to you, whatever things you ask when you pray, believe that you receive them, and you will have them.'" Mark 11:22-24

In the previous Scripture, Jesus is basically saying, "That mountain you are facing—I have already conquered it. Now YOU tell it to move!"

Grab ahold of your Beloved's hand, and leap with Him over the mountains. Think about that—leaping over mountains. Only God can do that, and with such ease! What mountain are you facing in your life right now? Nothing is too hard or impossible for God to see you through it with His love.

"Behold, I am the LORD, the God of all flesh. Is there anything too hard for Me?" Jeremiah 32:27

"Jesus said to him, 'If you can believe, all things are possible to him who believes.'" Mark 9:23

Jesus is going to see you through as you learn to grab ahold of Him and not let go. Mountains can and will be conquered in your life if you understand that your Beloved is with you. Love conquers all.

The hills in this verse represent personal issues that we deal with in our lives. They are not as intense as the mountains that we face, but they are still obstacles or hindrances that are standing in the way of sweet communion with Jesus. In my book, *Killing Lazarus: Discover Why The Enemy Is Trying To Take You Out And What You Can Do About It,* I teach how you can live with a heart that is healed and whole.

The good news is that just as Jesus leaps over the mountains, He skips over the hills. This is a picture, again, that nothing is too hard for the Lord. Will you let Him conquer your mountains of debt, disease in your body, depression or fear? Will you allow Jesus to skip over the hills of low self-esteem, grief, marriage issues, decisions to make, offense and the like?

To imagine Jesus leaping and skipping over the mountains

and hills that you are facing should not give you a sense that He doesn't care about what you are going through. Rather, it should make you feel that there is absolutely nothing in your life that His love, His power, His blood, His joy, and His presence cannot see you through.

He knows that the mountains and hills that you face are hard on you and difficult to work through. He is very compassionate, patient, and understanding, while at the same time, standing in your future beckoning you to come, because His love has already conquered all. You need to learn to lean into Him and listen for His voice (the voice of your Beloved), which will give you hope, calm your spirit and bring you joy—and He will embrace you with His loving arms.

LEARNING TO LEAN

The night before I wrote this next section, I had a vivid dream. I was in a small church, sharing on some of what I wrote about in this book. During the message, I asked everyone who felt that they wanted to live wholehearted for Jesus to come to the altar, and almost everyone ran forward. As I watched them pour out their hearts before God, I got on my knees and wept and wept for them. Beloved, wholehearted living for Jesus is what your heart has been searching for and longing for. You just have to learn to lean into Jesus. Do you remember this old song?

> *"The joy I can't explain filled my soul*
> *The day I made Jesus my King.*

*His blessed Holy Spirit is leading my way,
He's teaching, and I'm learning to lean.
Learning to lean,
Learning to lean,
I'm learning to lean on Jesus.
Finding more power than I've ever dreamed,
I'm learning to lean on Jesus.*

*Sad, brokenhearted, at an altar I knelt.
I found peace that was so serene.
And all that He asks is a childlike trust,
And a heart that is learning to lean.*

*There's a glorious victory, each day now for me.
I've found peace so serene.
He helps me with each task, if I'll only ask.
Every day now, I'm learning to lean."*

Learning To Lean written by John Stallings

As I mentioned earlier in this book, the apostle John knew how to *lean*.

"Now there was leaning on Jesus 'bosom one of His disciples, whom Jesus loved. Simon Peter therefore motioned to him to ask who it was of whom He spoke. Then, leaning back on Jesus 'breast, he said to Him, 'Lord, who is it?'" John 13:23-25

I find it fascinating that John had the audacity to lean as he did on Jesus. We can see from all the writings of this "apostle of love" that he lived assured and confident of Jesus' love for him.

For over three years, John watched closely as this passionate, miracle working, Son of God/Son of man changed the world. And then there was the heart of Jesus that was so welcoming, so inviting, so loving that John felt courageously comfortable enough to lay back on Jesus at the table. And Jesus received him. Jesus was, is and will always be the epitome of love.

Why was John so confident in the love that Jesus had for Him? You see, by "leaning" on Jesus (whether physically or as his heart yearned for Jesus), John was getting to know who Jesus was. And by getting to know who Jesus was, John found out who he was to Jesus—the one who Jesus loved! As I said before, five times in the book of John, he referred to himself as "the one who Jesus loved". That's incredible to me. And that kind of heart assurance comes from "leaning" on Jesus.

When you "learn to lean", not only will you encounter His amazing love, but He will also share His secrets with you. Jesus has many things He wants to tell you if you would simply lean in a little closer—close enough to hear His heartbeat for you, your family, and those around you. I'm telling you, He's waiting right now for you to lean into His heart.

If you want to feel His love, if you want to hear His voice, if you want to encounter the depths of His heart, if you want to know what He thinks and feels about you, then...

...*LEAN.*

So how do I lean? The secret is found in the abiding that we read about in John 15. Abide with Jesus as much as you can. Rest in His love. Meditate on His Word. Soak in His presence. Worship Him. Pray in tongues often. And be still and know that He is God.

"If you want that splendid power in prayer, you must remain in loving, living, lasting, conscious, practical, abiding union with the Lord Jesus Christ." Charles Spurgeon

PERSONAL APPLICATION

Jesus has already leapt over your mountains and skipped over your hills, because His love has conquered all for you through His death and resurrection. Now He wants you to grab hold of His hand to implement the victory in your life. What mountains and hills are still in your life where you need to see the victory as you learn to lean into Jesus?

_____
_____
_____
_____
_____
_____
_____
_____
_____
_____
_____
_____
_____
_____
_____
_____
_____
_____
_____
_____
_____

Living Loved

12

GAZING

"My beloved is like a gazelle or a young stag. Behold, he stands behind our wall; He is looking through the windows, gazing through the lattice." Song of Songs 2:9

In the previous chapter, we read that Jesus was leaping and skipping over mountains and hills. However, in this verse, we read that He is standing. I feel that there are times in our lives where we are leaping and skipping with Lord as we win victories together, but sometimes, He is simply standing at the door of our heart, longing to be invited to commune with us.

"Behold, I stand at the door and knock. If anyone hears My voice and opens the door, I will come in to him and dine with him, and he with Me." Revelation 3:20

This Scripture in Revelation is written to the church. It's written to you and me. If we would simply open the door and invite Him in, He would come in and dine with us. "Ryan, do you mean to say that all I have to do is open the door, and

He will come?" Yes, because that's what the Bible says! So many believers are waiting and waiting for a visitation from Jesus when He is right outside their door. He's just on the other side of the wall. He will stand at the door of your heart and knock and knock and knock, but He still has to be invited in. You have to go to the door and let Him in. I feel the presence of the Lord so strong as I write this. Jesus is longing for us to invite Him in. The door, or the wall, represents our hearts. We must open up our hearts to Him if we are going to experience His love, joy and peace.

"For the love which God bears to the soul, His eternal, never-ceasing desire to enter into it, and to dwell in it, stays no longer than till the door of the heart opens for Him. For nothing does, or can keep God out of the soul, or hinder His holy union with it, but the desire of the heart turned from Him." William Law

Think about it: King Jesus is standing at the door of your heart and speaking to you through the door. "Do you hear my voice? Do you realize I'm at the door? Are you too busy in the house for Me? I love you, son. I love you, daughter. Will you let me in?"

You see, although Jesus has conquered all (mountains and hills), He will not force Himself into your heart any more than you are willing to allow Him entrance. In this verse, it says that He is standing behind *our* wall. Did you catch that? It's *our* wall. We are the ones that put walls up between us and Jesus. You need to understand that we are the ones behind the wall, behind the door. Jesus is unhindered in His desire and pursuit of us. We are hindering Him; He's not hindering us.

These walls represent our self-protection and security, with which we tend to shut out the world, along with its problems and the needs of others. It's walls that keep us from taking risks with going deeper in God. Again, it represents the hindrances between us and Jesus.

We have put up walls in our lives because of what we have been through, how we were raised, trauma that has affected us, marriage struggles, financial burdens, disappointments, shame and the list goes on. What we don't realize is that those same walls have also kept Jesus out. Because of what has happened in our pasts, we put up walls that hinder intimacy with God, and this is one of the biggest reasons why some believers do not seem to encounter the love of God. They have a wall up that won't let love through. Jesus doesn't come to our hearts (I'm talking about after we are born again) and start kicking open doors and tearing down walls. Those areas have to be yielded to the Holy Spirit so He can perform a deep, cleansing, healing work within us.

Some of the walls that have been put up between us and God are lies that we have believed about God. The enemy is the one who gave us those thoughts, and they created a hindrance to receiving the good things that God has in store for us. The enemy has whispered, "God is not as good as you think He is. God has given up on you. You have gone too far.

God doesn't love you like you think He does. God is not for you. God was not there to help you through your hard season in life. God has let you down." Friend, these are all lies of the enemy that have to be dealt with, healed, and replaced with the truth of what God feels about you.

We sometimes make the mistake of thinking that Jesus is behind the wall, and we can't get to Him. Think about that. Picture yourself in your home. Now picture Jesus standing just outside your door or the wall of your home. Who is the one that is actually confined behind a wall? It's you, not Jesus! You are the one behind the walls and doors that you have built up throughout your entire life. Jesus is not the one that's confined, He's outside in the vast open space. You are the one that is sitting in your comfort zone and living in protection mode. This is why your relationship with the Lord is not at the place where you had hoped it would be at this point in your life. He loves you so much, but He will not force His way into your heart. Are you ready to yield to Him and tear down your walls?

In this Scripture, we see her Beloved looking through the windows, gazing through the lattice. I love the thought of that—the picture of Jesus looking and longing to be with His sons and daughters. Although we have these walls up, He still pursues us and is looking and gazing into our hearts (He always sees what's going on through your window—your heart). He has such a furious longing and love, desiring to come into our hearts in a deeper way.

He is gazing at us with eyes of love and joy. He gazes at us, and we don't even realize it. We go about our busy lives with our busy schedules, and He is gazing at us. He loves us so much. We are His precious children. Speaking of busy schedules:

"One reason we are so harried and hurried is that we make yesterday and tomorrow our business, when all that legitimately concerns us is today. If we really have too much to do, there are some items on the agenda which God did not put there. Let us submit the list to Him and ask Him to indicate which items we must delete. There is always time to do the will of God. If we are too busy to do that, we are too busy." Elisabeth Elliot

I know that as you are reading this, you are hearing the knock on your heart and feeling the gaze of His love. Will you let Him in? Are you willing to let Him in to challenge your current comfort zone of intimacy? His grace is sufficient to help you tear down your walls. He is longing to be invited to commune with you. He is patiently waiting. He is here right now.

Are you willing to host Jesus at your house—your heart? Are you ready to host His presence in the secret place of prayer? Jesus is looking for good hosts—those who will invite Him in, spend time with Him, and make Him feel welcome. And as He sits down with you and loves on you, He will share deep, beautiful, and loving revelations that will change the whole course of your life from the inside out!

"Abide in Me says Jesus. Cling to Me. Stick fast to Me. Live the life of close and intimate communion with Me. Get nearer to Me. Roll every burden on Me. Cast your whole weight on Me. Never let go your hold on Me for a moment. Be, as it were, rooted and planted in Me. Do this and I will never fail you. I will ever abide in you" J.C. Ryle

PERSONAL APPLICATION

Right now, Jesus is knocking at the door of your heart. ALL you have to do is open the door, and He will come and be with you. It is very important that you talk to Jesus about any walls that you have up in your heart that are keeping you from intimacy with God. If you ask the Holy Spirit to reveal to you why you are not a good receiver of God's love, He will show you. You may see a picture in your mind. You may have a vision. He may even bring something to your remembrance.

It's vitally important that you take your time, and be quiet before Him, so you will hear His voice. He is longing to speak to you. He is gazing at you right now with His compassionate heart. He created you, and you are His beloved child. One of the most important messages I'm trying to get across to you through this book is that you can encounter the love and presence of God for yourself. God is not leaving you out of His family. However, you MUST open the door of your heart. You have to let down your walls. You have gone this far in this book, and I am proud of you. Now, take another step toward the Lord today, and spend time abiding in His presence. I am believing with you that you will have a fresh encounter with Him! In the space provided, journal what took place today when you spent time with Jesus:

_____
_____
_____
_____

Living Loved

13

COME AWAY

"My beloved spoke, and said to me: 'Rise up, my love, my fair one, and come away.'" Song of Songs 2:10

This is such a loving call to a deeper place of intimacy from her Beloved. No matter what is going on in your life right now, you are "His love".

Jesus is speaking to *your* heart to *rise up*. He is speaking to you to rise up from complacency. Rise up from your brokenness. Rise up from religion, and enjoy relationship. He is saying, "Rise up from all that hinders love and intimacy, my love, and run away with Me."

I feel to remind you, dear reader, that all that I have written in this book is for every woman and every man. The Lord is speaking to *everyone* reading this to come to Him in a fresh, new way and enjoy the banqueting table of communion and love. For the rest of our lives, Jesus will call us closer and closer to His heart as we are on the journey to our heavenly home.

RELIGION VS. RELATIONSHIP

Beloved, it's one thing to know about God, but it's an entirely different thing to know God. It's religion vs. relationship. There is a vast difference between religion and relationship with our Father. Here's what religion is like (the following is taken from my book, *Carrying the Presence*):

"Religion is like trudging through the desert and seeing a mirage in the distance. It looks refreshing. It looks like water. But the closer you get, you are let down—it was only a mirage—it was just religion.

Religion is like running through a maze. You turn this way and that way, only to find another dead end. Religion in and of itself makes you feel hopeless and helpless.

Religion is like building a large, cold campfire. You have the logs and twigs set up just right for the perfect blaze. You set chairs around the area for everyone to enjoy. And that's it. You never light the campfire. Everything looks good and is prepared just right with all your friends, but there is no fire, no heat, no joy—just a cold campfire. That's religion. That's a lot of our churches today. Jesus did not come to earth to start a religion, but to bring us back to the Father.

You see, in our pursuit of God, religion will never satisfy. Only a deep, personal, intimate relationship with Jesus will bring the longings of a human heart to rest. From a distance, religion may look good, feel good, and sound good, but it's only a mirage of the real thing. Religion will keep getting us to pursue a mirage if we are not careful. So what do we do when our hearts are left unsatisfied and wanting because of religion?

People cannot truly know God without an intimate relationship with Him. Father never intended for us to have a one-sided relationship with Him. Remember reading what Adam had in the beautiful Garden of Eden, walking and talking with His Father? They enjoyed sweet communion together until sin entered the scene.

You see, the human heart was designed to live in Eden—in communion with the Father. Anything less simply does not satisfy. People on the journey of life in this 'dry and thirsty land' will many times settle for religion and not relationship. There is no true joy in religion, in and of itself. Religion, at best, is supposed to point us to a relationship with God.

It is in Him that we find an 'oasis' of divine fellowship and communion throughout each day. Father longs for you to encounter Him in this way. He has so much to show you and share with you. He wants to share His heart with you about what you are experiencing today and what you will face tomorrow." Carrying The Presence, Ryan Bruss

It's time for us all to rise up and seek the Lord like never before. I know that you are feeling the pull in your heart to go deeper in God. The Holy Spirit is speaking to you and wooing you to intimacy. You are His fair one, His beloved child. Begin to rise up today to run away from all that hinders love, and run toward His heart.

Jesus is saying, "Come away with Me. We have things to do together. I want to take you on an adventure. It's you and me together. I am bringing you to a new season in your life. Let me hold you. Let me love you. Let me heal you. Come away, My Beloved."

"How divinely full of glory and pleasure shall that hour be when all the millions of mankind that have been redeemed by the blood of the Lamb of God shall meet together and stand around Him, with every tongue and every heart full of joy and praise! How astonishing will be the glory and the joy of that day when all the saints shall join together in one common song of gratitude and love, and of everlasting thankfulness to this Redeemer! With that unknown delight, and inexpressible satisfaction, shall all that are saved from the ruins of sin and hell address the Lamb that was slain, and rejoice in His presence!" Isaac Watts

PERSONAL APPLICATION

Are you beginning to" rise up" and come away with your Beloved? Do you feel that there are areas in your life where you have been religious—saying and doing all the right things outwardly, but without a heart that's ignited with a passion and zeal for Jesus? This is a good time to repent for replacing relationship with religion and religious activities. When you are able to identify those religious areas, write them down so you can remember what to never go back to!

_____
_____
_____
_____
_____
_____
_____
_____
_____
_____
_____
_____
_____
_____
_____
_____
_____
_____
_____
_____

Living Loved

14

A NEW SEASON

"For lo, the winter is past, the rain is over and gone. The flowers appear on the earth; the time of singing has come, and the voice of the turtledove is heard in our land. The fig tree puts forth her green figs, and the vines with the tender grapes give a good smell. Rise up, my love, my fair one, and come away!" Song of Songs 2:11-13

Beloved, a new, glorious season is coming to your life! I have lived in Massachusetts, Illinois and Minnesota, so I am very familiar with the winter season. The wind chill in Minnesota one day was a frigid -50°. I remember kicking a chunk of ice off my car, and a large piece of my car fell off with the ice! I also built houses through the cold, bitter, winter months. We couldn't wait for the spring and summer to return.

Let me share with you for just a moment on the winter season, as mentioned in the opening verse of this chapter. Sometimes, when we are in the winter season of life, we feel like, "God, where are You? I can't feel Your presence. Have You left me alone? Do I have to go through this by myself? I feel so cold on the inside." We have all faced the winter seasons in our walk with God. But this season can be the greatest time of growth and maturity in our lives.

In the winter season, God is saying to us, "Keep seeking Me. Keep praying. Don't give up. Keep loving Me. Keep reading my Word. Keep running after Me. I am doing a deep work within your heart, and this is all going to be worth it! This difficult winter season will soon pass."

"The winter prepares the earth for the spring, so do afflictions sanctified prepare the soul for glory." Richard Sibbes

We go through brutal winter seasons for many different reasons. Sometimes it's an intense demonic attack. Sometimes it's a personal attack from someone you know. Sometimes it's Father God's intention to bring you into a new place in Him and a deeper revelation of His heart. Whatever the reason for the intense winter season in your life, you must still know that you are deeply loved. You can still live loved in the winter season. You must have the revelation of the depth of His love, even in the harsh winter season that you are going through.

It's Father's wonderful love that carries you through each season of life. That's why it's so important to always cultivate love with Jesus when things are going well in your life. Just as chipmunk will faithfully gather food for itself for the winter months, so we too gather together with the Lord in the secret place so that we are prepared for when the winter season comes. We don't want to find ourselves unprepared in the winter season because of a lack of communion with Jesus in the warm and joyful seasons of life.

In the winter seasons that we face, always remember that Jesus has not left you. You are not alone. He is, and will always be, close by your side. He remains faithful to you and will lead, guide, and help you through this season.

When you find yourself in a winter season, don't run from God. Run to Him. Run into His arms of love. In this season, remember the promises of God that He has given to you through His Word. Remember the prophetic words that have been spoken over your life. Through the pain, through the tears, through the darkness, keep pressing into His heart. You may feel like you can't go on, but the Holy Spirit is right there with you, encouraging you to stay the course.

The Lord just shared with me that that's a word for someone reading this:" Stay the course". In my spirit, I saw you on a boat, and the wind and the waves were violently coming against you. I saw you crying. I saw that you wanted to just give up. But then you felt hope rise within you—the hope that Father God has not left you or forsaken you, because you are loved. Then you hoisted up your sails and caught the wind, and it pulled you through the storm. Beloved, you are going to make it through this winter season. How can I be so sure? Because the winter season ALWAYS passes.

Spiritually speaking, I have been through many dark, cold, winter seasons, and I am sure you have as well. The greatest key to making it through these dark seasons is to have already established your heart in God *prior* to the winter season. There are many people that I know that have either backslidden or given up on living passionately for Jesus, and some have even fallen away from God, because they did not have their hearts anchored in the Father's love when they came into the winter season. If we keep our hearts continually in fellowship with Jesus, when the winter season comes, we don't lose our heart or our faith in God.

I am in no way saying that the winter season is easy to go through—not at all. As I said, I have been through many harsh winter seasons myself. What has gotten me through EVERY SINGLE TIME is the fact that my heart was rooted and grounded in His love (see Ephesians 3). That's how you make it through. That's how I made it through—by ALWAYS staying close to Jesus through prayer, worship, praying in tongues and staying in His Word regularly.

As I write this chapter, it's almost the end of spring here in North Carolina. The leaves are fully back on the trees. The flowers that my wife planted all around the house are in bloom. The weather is beautiful and warm. There is new life all around us. This is spring. And this is what happens when Father does a new thing in your life. Spiritually speaking, this is what happens in our lives after the winter season is gone. Beloved, Father is doing a new thing in you!

"Do not remember the former things, nor consider the things of old. Behold, I will do a new thing, now it shall spring forth; shall you not know it? I will even make a road in the wilderness and rivers in the desert." Isaiah 43:18-19

PERSONAL APPLICATION

I'm sure that you have been through winter seasons in your life. What did your heart feel like in those seasons? How were you responding to God? How were you responding to others? What did you learn? How did the winter seasons affect you emotionally, physically, spiritually or even financially? The reason why I am asking you these questions is because the next time you face a winter season in your life, I want your heart to be prepared. When we live rooted and grounded in Father's love, His love will see us through. Based on what you are learning so far, what steps can you take in your life to keep your heart rooted and grounded in God so that you never give up, you never backslide and you never walk away from God? In the space provided, write down how you are going to keep your heart anchored in God from this moment on. Keep in mind that you *already* are Father's child. So, it's not about trying to be a son or daughter. It's about anchoring your heart in Him:

_____
_____
_____
_____
_____
_____
_____
_____
_____
_____

Living Loved

15

THE SECRET PLACE OF HIS LOVE

"O my dove, in the clefts of the rock, in the secret places of the cliff, let me see your face, let me hear your voice; for your voice is sweet, and your face is lovely."
Song of Songs 2:14

The secret place of His love—this is where we encounter His beauty, love, joy, peace, majesty, power—you name it. The secret place of His love is where we meet with God and hear His voice speak beautiful revelations to our hearts.

The clefts of the rock and the cliff do not seem like very welcoming places to meet with God, but your Beloved Jesus wants to meet you right where you are at. He wants to see your lovely face. He wants to hear your sweet voice. Beauty is in the eye of the beholder, and you are the one that God is beholding. He loves you. He likes you. He enjoys you. He created you, and He loves everything that He has created. You are not a mistake. You are not the black sheep of God's family. He longs for you to gaze back at Him. He longs for you to talk to Him. God is powerful, strong, mighty, and has all authority, but He is also tender, kind, loving, and merciful.

Friend, each one of us still has areas in our lives that we are walking out and coming into maturity in, yet He still deeply loves and cares for us. Living our lives before God is not about living perfectly, but living in a way that is pleasing to Him. And if we live to please Him, we will do those things that He has commanded us to do.

"Therefore you shall be perfect, just as your Father in Heaven is perfect." Matthew 5:48

I am not a scholar by any means, but from my study, this word "perfect" means "complete or coming into maturity". Someone once illustrated this verse, defining the word "perfect" like the old sea captain's telescope, unfolding (extending out) one stage at a time to eventually function at full-strength. It's growing in grace. Growing in love. Growing in maturity and continually allowing the Holy Spirit to help us remove all that is in the way of living daily in His presence.

Do I believe that in this life we can attain this level of maturity? Yes, it is possible by God's grace. Otherwise, Jesus would have never commanded us to do it. Jesus NEVER asks us to do anything that He has not given us the power and grace to accomplish. However, few are willing to pay the price to be that close to Jesus and that free of self-will.

"Deep calls unto deep at the noise of Your waterfalls; all Your

waves and billows have gone over me." Psalm 42:7

So, when the Bible talks about being perfect, I believe it is encouraging us to go to deeper and deeper levels of maturity in God. However, I see many believers trying to be perfect before God as defined by Webster's dictionary. **Perfect:** *Having no mistakes or flaws, completely correct or accurate. Being entirely without fault or defect.* Beloved, Jesus was the only One that has ever lived perfectly.

So then, why is it that within our heart of hearts, we are trying to be perfect (as defined by Webster) before God? Why would we strive for something that's not possible to attain? Why do we set ourselves up for continual failure?

I had the privilege of coaching baseball and basketball for a number of years. Coaching kids' sports is no picnic, let me tell you. But it teaches (the coach as well as players) valuable lessons if hearts are open. As a coach, you can fall into the temptation to expect kids to play perfectly all the time. A young player may strike out in baseball and walk back to the dugout crying because he wanted to hit the ball perfectly every time. It's not going to happen. The kid put tremendous pressure on himself for something he will never do—hit the ball EVERY TIME. I tried to tell the players that even in the major leagues, the good hitters only hit the ball a third of the time. It's the same with us on a daily basis. Our hearts want to hit a (spiritual) home run every day, and when it doesn't happen, we immediately beat ourselves up as we head back to the dugout and cry on the bench.

We do not walk in perfect love every day. That alone is humbling. We do not have a perfect prayer life. We do not have a perfect thought life. We do not have a perfect response in every situation that we face. We are not mistake free and flawless. We are not completely correct or accurate. We are not entirely without fault or defect.

Read about the "heroes" of the faith again in Hebrews 11. Read about Moses the murderer, Jacob the deceiver, Joseph the proud, Rahab the harlot, Gideon the fearful, Samson the weak, and David the adulterer, and you will realize that God deeply loves His *imperfect* ones.

> *"Imperfection is the prerequisite for grace. Light only gets in through the cracks." Philip Yancey*

So, what do we do? Do we live however we want, and God will say, "Oh well, he/she is not perfect!"? Certainly not. This is not God's heart. What we do first is take a deep breath and realize that we are imperfect people living in an imperfect world. Therefore, we will make mistakes. We will fall short. We will sin.

So then, what do we do? We live to *please* God in every area of our lives. There is a vast difference between living *perfect* and living to *please* God. Jesus said it so beautifully in John 8:29:

"And He who sent Me is with Me. The Father has not left Me alone, for I always do those things that please Him."

Here's the truth that will awaken your heart: You see, trying to live perfect is fear-based. We may not admit it, but we can be subtly afraid that if we don't act right, think right and do everything perfectly that God will get mad at us and turn away from us. This brings tremendous shame and reveals doubts of Father God's true feelings for us. We tend to lean more toward the thought that He is continually disappointed with us, rather than toward His tremendous love for us. We tend to think that because we are surprised by our sin and weaknesses, God is also. But He is not.

To live to please God is love-based. It's a heart that desires and strives to live with authenticity, because it *pleases* Him. It's a heart that desires to be pure and clean before Him, because we love Him and we know this brings Him pleasure. This is what the Bible means about being perfect. It's to grow in the things of God—to grow and mature in our love for God and others. The more we tap into His love, the more the desire to please Him will follow. To know His love is to know what pleases Him. Our sin does not please Him—of course not. But a heart that desires to live pure and holy every day— that pleases Him deeply.

I would often coach my own son, whether it was in baseball or basketball. He is my son, and I love him with all my heart, but he did not play perfectly—although he tried. When I would be on the sidelines watching/coaching the game, no matter how he played, he was first and foremost, my son. Whether he made a free throw or got a base hit or not, it did not change that fact that he was my son. No matter what his performance was like in a game, I certainly did not stop loving or enjoying him.

My son, Andrew, continues to play baseball in his late teens and aspires to one day play Major League Baseball. At the time of this writing, he has another game this weekend. If you were to ask Andrew what his Dad has taught him about stepping up to the plate each time or stepping out in the field each inning, he would say, "My dad has taught me that no matter what happens in the game, I have already won, because I have won God's heart," That's embedded in Andrew's heart. My son has had many defensive plays that have caused the people watching to loudly cheer. He has also had the baseball roll past his glove in a clutch moment. Andrew has had "walk off" hits to win big games and has also been at the plate where he had the chance to win the game, but struck out. His highs and lows on the baseball field do not change my love and adoration for him in anyway whatsoever. Yes, he works hard to be the best that he can be, as my daughter also does with her college equestrian team, but no matter what their performance ends up looking like, he's my son, and she's my daughter!

Father God is not keeping a tally of the ups and downs of your life to determine His level of love for you today. Not at all. Father loves you at your lowest moment as much as He loves you at your best. You are a child of God, His creation. That alone brings Him tremendous joy, love and adoration for you.

As I write this paragraph, my daughter is competing at an equestrian event. At the last event, a couple of weeks prior, she won reserve champion out of a large class of competitors. This weekend, she may not win anything at all, but that does not change my love and adoration for who she is—my beloved daughter. Incidentally, when my wife and I wanted to have children, I asked God for a daughter first. He gave us Elianna which means, "My God has answered."

My kids are the joy of my heart, and the love I have for them is greater than their ability to do everything perfectly. As parents, we have to fight the temptation to expect our kids to do everything perfectly 24/7. Give them some space, and let your love for them shine through.

A few years ago, I was at my niece's high school graduation. I think there were about three thousand people in attendance, including the students. At the beginning of the ceremony, someone made an announcement about everyone in the audience holding applause and cheers until the end so that they could quickly get through all the names of those graduating. I will never forget, as long as I live, what happened next. About a third of the way through the ceremony, the name of one of the graduating students was called, and from the other side of the auditorium, a father yelled out, "THAT'S MY BOY!" It was so loud and clear and heartfelt. It touched me deeply. What a proud dad! It brings tears to my eyes reliving the moment in my heart as I write this story.

Father God feels the same way about you as He looks your way. He says, "That's my boy! That's my girl!". You have captured the heart of God, my friends. You are His sons and daughters. Don't ever let the enemy tell you anything different!

"My deepest awareness of myself is that I am deeply loved by Jesus Christ and I have done nothing to earn it or deserve it." Brennan Manning

Even in God's discipline, we can encounter His love.

"And you have forgotten the exhortation which speaks to you as to sons: 'My son, do not despise the chastening of the LORD, nor be discouraged when you are rebuked by Him; for whom the LORD loves He chastens, and scourges every son whom He receives.'" Hebrews 12:5-6

When God disciplines us, it's truly a sign of His love. Some may say, "Then He must REALLY love me." Me too! Just as we discipline our own kids, the Lord will discipline us. His discipline always leads us into greater measures of communion and love when we learn the sometimes painful lessons that He is teaching us.

Always remember that divine correction is not rejection; it's love. When we learn from those mistakes and sins that we commit and those things that do not please God, we wage war against doing those same things again. Just know that He is very forgiving. God is a perfect Father. He is 100% love and 100% just at the same time.

We need to learn to live out of our identity of being a son or a daughter before a Father that loves us so deeply and profoundly. You are a son first! You are a daughter first! And He loves you so much. You are His favorite. You don't have a rebellious heart (and if you do, this is your moment to repent and make things right with God!), but rather, you are an imperfect son or daughter with a passionate heart for Jesus.

Live to please Him. Live to love Him. Live to know Him. Mature in the things of God. Mature in your love for God and others. This is being perfect as the Bible defines it. Live to please the Lord in all that you say and do; this pleases His heart more than you will never know.

"Nothing binds me to my Lord like a strong belief in His changeless love." C. H. Spurgeon

PERSONAL APPLICATION

Father God loves your heart. You are His special treasure. Just the fact that you are His creation brings Him great joy! I know that you want to please the Father's heart. Jesus said that He always did those things that please His Father. What are some of the ways that, through your own life, you can do those things that please the Father? Write them here:

___
___
___
___
___
___
___
___
___
___
___
___
___
___
___
___
___
___
___
___
___
___
___

Living Loved

Living Loved

16

LITTLE FOXES

"Catch us the foxes, the little foxes that spoil the vines, for our vines have tender grapes." Song of Songs 2:15

Driving to work one day, many years ago, I stopped off for some breakfast to go. When I got back into my car to take a bite of food, I smelled the familiar strong scent of an air freshener that my wife had put under the seats. Well, I couldn't take that smell any longer (it had been in the car for several days), so I threw the air freshener out my door. As soon as I did that, I heard the voice of the Lord so clearly say, "It's the little foxes that spoil the vine." Convicted, I got out of my car and picked up the air freshener that had blown under my car in that middle area that's hard to reach.

Foxes are quick, subtle, crafty animals that are hard to catch. They come to take away the intimate communion that we share with Jesus. What do these foxes represent to us? They are the areas of compromise that hold us back from deeper experiences in our journey of knowing God. The foxes are after our vines, which represent our lifeline to Jesus.

"I am the vine, you are the branches. He who abides in Me, and I in him, bears much fruit; for without Me you can do nothing." John 15:5

Those little foxes represent everything in our lives that hinder intimacy between us and Jesus. They could be a myriad of things, to be honest. And we have to "catch" them before they "spoil the vine". Those "foxes" could be the more subtle sins like bad attitudes, quick tempers, being irritable, gossiping, etc. And of course, lust, hate, unforgiveness, pride and the like.

"Were we to permit to remain even the tiniest little sin which we know our conscience has condemned, we instantly would lose that perfect fellowship with God." Watchman Nee

Foxes are said to be cunning, mischievous, and shrewd. That sounds like the way sin tries to come and steal our hearts and minds away from God. Satan was cunning from the very beginning with Adam and Eve, and his tactics have not changed.

We are to live connected to the Vine—Jesus—because this is where we experience the divine flow of intimacy. And it's in this intimacy where we find the peace of God, the joy of the Lord, the love of the Father and every other good and perfect thing that comes from Him (see James 1:17).
If we allow the foxes to come in and spoil the vine, it will affect our relationships with the Lord. That doesn't mean

that He loves us less or has forsaken us, but that the divine flow from "vine to branch and branch to vine" will not be there. Thanks be to God that He is patient with us, but we have to be quick to repent of all that hinders so we do not block the flow of intimacy.

We catch the foxes by saying no to sin and yes to God. The Bible says that if we submit to the Father and resist the devil, the devil will flee (see James 4:7). Plain and simple. It's not complicated; it's a choice. It always comes down to a choice. Temptation needs your cooperation for it to become sin. Our desire for a beautiful, powerful, wonderful, passionate, amazing, joyful, intimate relationship with Jesus must outweigh our appetite for sin. And the beautiful thing is, God Himself has given us the power to resist sin! We don't have to go at this alone. We can lean on Him in our times of temptation, and He will deliver us out of each and every one of them as we yield to His Spirit.

"No temptation has overtaken you except such as is common to man; but God is faithful, who will not allow you to be tempted beyond what you are able, but with the temptation will also make the way of escape, that you may be able to bear it." 1 Corinthians 10:13

As we go deeper in God, we begin to realize that it's the little things that keep us back from experiencing more of Him and that try to sabotage our fruitfulness in life and ministry (spoiling the vine). You already know what some of those things are. First and foremost, it's those top few things that you know the Holy Spirit has already been dealing with you about. Start with those areas. If you are willing to listen, the Holy Spirit will show you those foxes in your life that need to be caught and dealt with.

"The love of Christ both wounds and heals, it fascinates and frightens, it kills and makes alive, it draws and repulses. There can be nothing more terrible or wonderful than to be stricken with love for Christ so deeply that the whole being goes out in a pained adoration of His person, an adoration that disturbs and disconcerts while it purges and satisfies and relaxes the deep inner heart." A. W. Tozer

PERSONAL APPLICATION

Beloved, are there any areas in your life that you know the Holy Spirit is dealing with you about that are "little foxes"? Let's take care of all that is trying to spoil the vine. Take the time now, and ask the Holy Spirit to show you any areas in your life where you have been allowing these foxes to have their way. In the space provided, write down those areas that the Holy Spirit is dealing with you about:

_____
_____
_____
_____
_____
_____
_____
_____
_____
_____
_____
_____
_____
_____
_____
_____
_____
_____
_____
_____

Living Loved

17

AWAKENED TO LOVE

"Refuse to be average. Let your heart soar as high as it will." A.W. Tozer

The greatest desire of my heart as you are going through this book is that your own heart is being awakened to the reality of the Father's love. I want you to live out of the same revelation that the apostle John did, who boldly proclaimed, "I am the one that Jesus loves!"

This confidence and assurance that we are living in the love of the Father is our divine inheritance as children of God. The enemy has tried and tried to get you to misunderstand the heart of God by giving you misinformation about what God thinks and feels about you. One of the greatest ways that we overcome the enemy's lies is by meditating on not only *who* God is, but *how* He feels about us.

"Believe God's love and power more than you believe your own feelings and experiences. Your rock is Christ, and it is not the rock that ebbs and flows but the sea." Samuel Rutherford

When we live out of the truth of Father's heart for us, it assures us that we can always run to Him and receive from His heart the good things that He has for us.

So, how do these truths become realities in our heart? We must take the time to be with Him on a regular basis. The prayer life of a Christian should not always feel like using a sledgehammer to break up large rocks. There are times when we go to God in prayer, and it's real warfare because of what we are going through. It's what the old saints of God referred to as " praying through". This is an important key to receiving our breakthrough. However, this should not always be how we are led in prayer. There must be times of sitting still before Him (like under the shade tree that we talked about) and receiving from Heaven. It's difficult to be in receiving mode when you are constantly talking to God when you pray. Learn to receive by being quiet and opening your heart to Him on a regular basis.

My friend, there truly is no substitute for the Father's love. Nothing on this earth can compare to His unfailing love. Just a moment in His love and presence can change your life forever. However, the enemy has tried to make us think that living the Christian life is too difficult—too difficult to love and serve a God that we don't necessarily see. The enemy will try confusing us through circumstances, by challenging our love and commitment to God, and by creating scenarios in our lives where we begin to even doubt God. The enemy will try to do all of this and more to keep us from pursuing the Father's heart.

I am sharing all this with you because it's time that we mature in our walk with God. It's time that we settle the issue within our hearts, once and for all, that Father God is a good and loving Father who has mapped out our lives for us, who loves us with all of His heart, who is for us and not against us—no matter what is happening around us—and who can be fully taken at His Word.

One of the keys to receiving from Father is to continually come to Him as little children (see Matthew 18:3), and that principle will never change. Children easily receive from God. Children trust their parents for everything. Children know how to run to their dad or mom when they get hurt or are having a difficult time with something. It's the same with our own Father in Heaven. There is nothing that He can't handle in your life. When we live in the reality of being incredibly loved, it's easier to go to God and say, "Help!".

In just a moment, I am going to teach you, practically, how to live loved every day. The personal application sections that I wrote for you at the end of the previous chapters were to prepare you for what I am about to share.

But first, I want you to take a good, long look at your life right now. How well are you prioritizing your relationship with God? Beloved, you can't ignore God throughout your days, weeks and months and expect to encounter Him like you want. Your relationship with God is your life-source, and the sooner that you understand that, the better. My dear friend, Dr. Kevin Zadai, has taught me in recent years the great and wonderful things that can happen to the believer whose life is completely sold out to Jesus. Nothing can take the place of your prayer life and the joy of daily practicing the presence of God wherever you go. To continually be aware within our hearts of the nearness of God changes the way we live our lives each day. Don't you want more of Him? Don't you want to encounter His presence? Don't you want to live loved? Then you must seek Him with ALL your heart—there simply is no other way.

I am telling you the truth. I have been a Christian now for over forty years, and I can tell you firsthand that there is NO OTHER WAY to experience the depths of God than to seek Him will all of our hearts. Even now, my heart is stirred to run to the secret place and pour out my love and worship to Him. Beloved, the truth is, just the very fact that we are born-again—just that alone—should keep us loving and adoring Him 24/7. Just the fact that one day soon, we will be with Him forever, should keep us pressing into His heart.

The enemy wants to rob you of these simple truths and create havoc in your life so you are too discouraged, offended, wounded, worn out, burned out and selfish to enjoy your relationship with God. If you give the enemy an inch, he will take a mile. He doesn't like you. He is not for you; he's against you. He wants to disrupt your life to the point that you leave your faith altogether. But that won't happen to you if you live in Father's love.

"Satan is ever seeking to inject that poison into our hearts to distrust God's goodness - especially in connection with his commandments. That is what really lies behind all evil, lusting and disobedience. A discontent with our position and portion, a craving from something which God has wisely held from us. Reject any suggestion that God is unduly severe with you. Resist with the utmost abhorrence anything that causes you to doubt God's love and his loving-kindness toward you. Allow nothing to make you question the Father's love for his child." A.W. Pink

Beloved, there are endless encounters awaiting those whose hearts long for more of God. I can see it so clearly in my spirit right now. The only thing that is holding you back from experiencing more and more of God is yourself. You are solely responsible for your own walk with God. You must hunger and thirst for God if you expect to be filled (see Matthew 5:6).

NOW TO LIVE THE LIFE

Are you ready to live loved? In this book, I have said over and over again what Father God thinks about you. And as we read in Psalm 139, the thoughts that He has toward us are greater than we could ever imagine. We just have to receive those wonderful thoughts deep into our hearts. When we do that, we live out of His thoughts for us.

The very first place you may need to start is with repentance. Ask the Holy Spirit to reveal to you all those things that you have allowed to come between you and God. Remember that His blood washes away every sin. The enemy loves to remind us of our past, but once we repent, it's covered in the blood of Jesus. There is no need to remember your sins, because God does not remember them (see Isaiah 43:25). So, if you feel that there is ANYTHING coming between you and God, bring it to Him, and repent of it. And always remember to keep your heart pure before Him. Don't let any secret sin become hidden within your heart. God forgives EVERY sin. That means secret sins and sins that other people may be aware of in us. He forgives everything. When we repent, it's by faith in His Word that we have received forgiveness.

After you repent, if you still feel too dirty or unclean to receive His love and enjoy fellowship with Him, you have to go to that place in your heart, and ask God to heal you so you can receive forgiveness. If you are like me, you may tend to be hard on yourself. In the past, I have had trouble forgiving myself, so I had to learn to trust in His Word, receive His Word and apply His Word to my life. Remember, it's not about what you feel at the moment; it's what His Word says. As you can read from the heart of David in Psalm 51, sin makes you feel unclean. It's only through Jesus that we can be forgiven, cleansed, and made whole. Why am I sharing all this with you? Because you won't be able to go far in God if you don't know how to receive forgiveness for the things you have done. So, it's first things first.

"If we confess our sins, He is faithful and just to forgive us our sins and to cleanse us from all unrighteousness." 1 John 1:9

Did you catch that? ALL unrighteousness. Now, if you do what this verse says and receive its truth, everything is going to be alright. Whatever it is that you have done, it has now been dealt with. Forgive yourself as well. You are clean before God. In my spirit, I see someone crying tears of relief, joy and hope, because you are receiving these truths of His love and forgiveness for you. And I believe others will see a change in you like in this quote from D.L. Moody:

"When Christ was on the earth there was a woman in the temple who was bowed almost to the ground with sin. Satan had bound her for eighteen years; but after all these years of bondage Christ delivered her. He spoke one word and she was free. She got up and walked home. How astonished those at home must have been to see her walking in." D. L. Moody

To live loved, you want to make sure your identity (the real you) is rooted and grounded in the truth of Father's heart for you. As a pastor, I have worked with many people who have had a false identity about themselves for many different reasons. Many, many people that I meet struggle with identity issues. I have briefly touched on this already, but in these closing chapters, it's important that you are reminded that how you feel and think about yourself *will* affect how you live before God and others.

Aren't you tired of trying to be someone that you're not? Aren't you tired of feeling unloved, overlooked, and like you're just a shell of who you want to be? Aren't you tired of your heart living in survival mode? Aren't you tired of feeling bad about yourself?

Through the years, our identities have been shaped by how we were raised, what we've done or what's been done to us and how we have processed information that we have received into our lives since we were born. The good news is that Father God wants to have His truth written upon our identities. The bad news is that the devil wants his lies to replace God's truth about us.

How we see ourselves and how we feel about ourselves must line up with how God sees us and feels about us. Having His truths written on our hearts is how we correctly process who we really are in this world. And at the core of who we are, if we remove all the lies the enemy has fed us through the years, we will each find that person (who we really are) that is wholeheartedly loved, adored, and enjoyed by God. That's the reality we should be living in every day. When we live in that reality, we don't succumb to the lies of the enemy or what anyone in this world thinks or feels about us.

I don't know what you have been through in life, but to live loved, you're going to need to identify any area in your life where you have buried hurts and wounds within your heart. Father's love is available to heal even the deepest trauma that you have been through. The key to wholeness is to yield those areas to God, forgive those who have hurt you, receive healing of all damaged emotions and replace them with truth from the Word of God. This is a process, so I'm not saying it's easy, but when you give your pain and sorrow to God, He is more than willing to take it from you and replace it with His heart for you.

I have done this very thing for myself. In the last chapter of this book, I have provided many Scriptures that you can use to renew your mind with truth from the Word of God. When your identity is in the right place, it's much easier to receive the Father's love.

For instance, let's take the Scripture found in Psalm 43:5, *"Why are you cast down, O my soul? And why are you disquieted within me? Hope in God; for I shall yet praise Him, the help of my countenance and my God."*

Take this Scripture, find a quiet place to pray, and meditate on this wonderful verse. You can pray something like, "Father, show me why my soul is cast down. What is bothering me? What is troubling my heart? Why do I feel beaten down and discouraged all the time? Why do I feel so much turmoil and restlessness in my heart? Jesus, forgive me for lashing out at others for what is an issue within my own heart. Holy Spirit, show me the areas in my heart that have not been yielded or healed that are causing me to be downcast. O Father, teach me to put my hope in You! Teach me to wait on You. Show me how to trust You with all my heart. You are my hope. You are my source. I don't put any hope in the things of this world. Father, I now realize that my hope has been shaken because of what I have gone through. I see that now. Father, I praise You right now. I worship You. Fill me with Your presence. Fill me with Your love. I receive Your love for me. You are my help. You are my hope. Satan, you no longer have a foothold in my life in this area. In Jesus name, I replace the lies and the torment with the truth of God's Word over me. Father, thank You for refreshing my heart as I renew my mind with the truth that You truly are my hope and my help. Amen."

It's time to be honest with yourself. You don't want to go year after year holding on to issues in your heart. The example prayer and Scripture that I gave you can be applied to any area of your heart where your identity has not been renewed. Use one of the Scriptures from the back of this book, or find one for yourself, and meditate and pray those verses back to God until you see breakthrough. It's not about repeating a verse hundreds of times for it to become a reality in your spirit. That's fine to do that, but it's more about receiving the revelation of God's Word over you and living out of that truth each day.

Sometimes people are waiting for outside circumstances to change before they will work on their hearts. I have seen this time and time again with believers. For instance, when their finances are good, they are happy and doing well. When their finances are not so good, they crumble and wonder why God doesn't care about their needs.

Most of the time, the way we respond to the negative things that happen to us outwardly will reveal to us if our hearts are anchored in Jesus or not. Everyone goes through tests, trials and temptations, but these things don't have to cause us to give up, give in, or lose our faith. Study the Scriptures over and over again so your heart is only anchored in God and not in the things of this world. We MUST quit reading the Word of God from a perspective that the Scriptures don't work for us. Nothing could be further from the truth. God is not a liar. He is not mocked. He has always been true to His Word. When are you going to start believing that? All the Scriptures I have shared with you throughout this book about Father's love can be applied to your own heart. Beloved, everything I am telling you has all worked to bring great changes in my own life.

There have been many areas in my own life where I have had to apply all of these principles, because my identity did not line up with how God felt about me. The enemy knows how to take the bad things that have happened to us and twist them in such a way that we feel abandoned and unloved by God.

Now, I don't sit around wondering day after day if there are areas in my heart that still need to be dealt with. Here's what I do: if something comes up in my life where I overreact in a situation, or I do something totally "out of character", or I sin in a certain area—whatever the case may be—these are red flags that tell me that there may be something deeper in my heart that I need to go to God and take care of. It's not a condemning situation (not that it feels good in the moment), but a chance to take care of something in my own heart that will bring me to an even deeper place of love, commitment, and intimacy with Jesus. And Father's love is always available to walk me through my shortcomings. I can tell you this: I do ask the Lord to show me any areas in my life that do not please Him so that there is nothing hindering any opportunity for me to encounter more and more of Him.

"An honest heart seeks to please God in all things and offend Him in none." A. W. Pink

Finally, as we come to the end of this book together, I want to share with you something else that I have done through the years that started me on this awakened journey of love and keeps my heart anchored in Him on a daily basis. I have learned to keep myself daily in the love of God. And the way we keep ourselves in Father's love is to keep our hearts *basking in His love* throughout the day. Jude 1:21 tells us:

"[K]eep yourselves in the love of God…"

We experience the joy of *living loved* when we keep ourselves *in His love* throughout the day. This takes practice, but it is so rewarding.

In my twenties, when I first went on my journey to learn how to love God and receive His love, I had to start at the beginning and search the Scriptures diligently to find what the Word said about His love. I read and meditated on these verses over and over and over again until they became part of me. Mike Bickle calls it the "beholding and becoming" principle. I have applied it to studying the heart of God, and it has worked wonders for me. Mike takes this principle from the following verse:

"But we all, with unveiled face, beholding as in a mirror the glory of the Lord, are being transformed into the same image from glory to glory, just as by the Spirit of the Lord." 2 Corinthians 3:18

In essence, Mike Bickle teaches that whatever we behold in God, we become—and that is what transforms our hearts. When I understood this principle and applied it to my life in the area of the love of the Father, that's when everything began to shift for me. I constantly would behold the love of God through prayer, meditation, worship, studying, fasting, healing of the heart, praying in tongues, more prayer, more meditation, more worship, more studying, more beholding—and the next thing I knew, I was becoming what I as beholding! I was becoming loved! I could see it. I could feel it. I was encountering His love. I get so excited just thinking about those early years of tapping into the love of God. Friends, beholding Father's love transformed me, and I became the one that Jesus loved! It transformed my entire outlook on my life—inside and out! Father's love has forever changed this formerly brokenhearted man. I am a living testimony of someone that lives loved. Incidentally, I have taken this same principle and have also applied it to many other areas of my walk with God.

Now, in my late forties, I still behold His love. I am still doing all those things that I did in the early years, because there is still so much more to encounter in God. I am still becoming more and more of what I am beholding. I am still being transformed by His love. I try to meditate on His love and goodness throughout each day, and this keeps me in the love of God.

I want my life to be used to help others come to know the love of the Father. Beloved, meditate on God as much as you can throughout the day.

"But his delight is in the law of the LORD, and in His law he meditates day and night. He shall be like a tree planted by the rivers of water, that brings forth its fruit in its season, whose leaf also shall not wither; and whatever he does shall prosper." Psalm 1:2-3

As you will see in the next chapter, I gave you many personal experiences that I have had with God in the secret place of prayer. All of those things that you are going to read flowed from my own heart and time spent with Jesus. But they are reminders of just some of what is awaiting you as your heart is awakened on this journey of love.

I love you, dear one. But more than that, Father God loves you with all of His heart. He is beckoning you to come and spend time with Him, and He will reveal Himself to you. He is waiting if you are willing.

When I reread this manuscript before it was published, my own heart was drawn closer to the Father! That's how I know that this book has come from Father God's heart to your heart. We are on this journey together.

"Measure not God's love and favour by your own feeling. The sun shines as clearly in the darkest day as it does in the brightest. The difference is not in the sun, but in some clouds which hinder the manifestation of the light thereof." Richard Sibbes

Live loved.

18

SITTING AT THE FEET OF JESUS

"Of all things, guard against neglecting God in the secret place of prayer." William Wilberforce

Beloved, get into the practice of sitting at the feet of Jesus every day, even if it's just for five minutes. The more we do this, the more we encounter His love, peace, power, joy, presence and everything else that our hearts are longing for on a regular basis. Resist all the ways the enemy is trying to keep you from sitting at His feet.

There are infinite possibilities that can happen when we cultivate a lifestyle of sitting at the feet of Jesus. I have listed for you just some of the *benefits and blessings* that we can experience when sitting at His feet (I personalized them for you):

>It's a place where I can always go.

Living Loved

It does not matter the time, space or place.

I am always welcome there.

I am never too ugly, fat, skinny or dirty to be welcome.

My Father is always there.

It's where my sadness is turned to joy.

All my sins are forgiven there.

It's a place of rest.

My strongholds are destroyed there.

It's where answers are given.

It's where I lay down my burdens and pick up His.

It's where my heart is healed.

My past is not only forgiven, but forgotten there.

I am never alone there.

I can laugh there.

I can dance there.

I can sing there, and no one ever cares if I am out of tune.

Living Loved

It's where the crooked places are made straight, and the rough places are made smooth.

The cares of the world seem to melt away there.

I can share my heart there and never ever feel ashamed or embarrassed.

At His feet, I am allowed to share my deepest feelings.

I can cry at His feet.

I can spend hours and hours there—or sometimes just five minutes.

I always feel stronger and happier when I leave.

Demons cannot dwell there.

I can get lost there—for hours.

Time stands still there.

Life can wait until I am through spending time at His feet.

Worry and confusion are not allowed entrance there.

Love surrounds me there.

I am not condemned there, though I may be gently reminded of things that need to change.

Living Loved

I can be myself there.

I remove the cloak of heaviness and put on the garment of praise.

I am continually reminded of God's precious promises there.

He reminds me there that everything in His Word is for me.

I can talk about others there, and pray for them, and not feel like I am gossiping.

I feel so protected there.

It's such a wonderful place of peace and rest for my soul.

It's a place where we talk about our future plans together.

It's a place of worship and praise.

Jesus can't wait until I get there.

It's where I am filled to overflowing with the presence of God.

I can let down my guard there.

It's where I can receive my orders for the day or plans for my future.

I can get my peace back there.

Living Loved

I do not have to pretend there; I can always be real.

It's where I can pull up to the table of the Lord, and all of Heaven meets me there.

Every time I sit at His feet, I leave changed.

I come out lighter every time, because more of the flesh has died.

I am fed there with the Bread of Heaven.

I can take communion with Jesus there.

He always reminds me there that I am His special child.

It's where my mind is renewed.

It's where my soul is refreshed.

It's where my spirit is strengthened.

It's where my heart is ignited with His fire.

It's a place where even though I may not "feel" anything at times, I know that He is always there with me.

I am challenged there.

I make fresh commitments there and not empty promises.

I can rest in the loving arms of Jesus there.

He does not call me servant there, but friend.

Living Loved

I can unashamedly abandon myself to Him there.

I can hear His loving voice there.

I feel like I am the only one in the world that He is paying attention to when I'm there, because He makes me feel welcome and secure.

All my tears are wiped away there.

My heart seems to always be stronger for Him when I leave.

When I am at His feet, I know that everything is going to be alright.

No one but us understands what takes place there.

I fall in love with Jesus more every time I'm there.

I am never too busy to sit at His feet.

Though I may fail at times, I am never looked at as a failure there.

This place with Jesus puts a longing in my heart for my next visit.

It's a place that I am pursuing to live in every moment of every day.

It's where I can soar on eagles' wings.

Living Loved

It's where the Holy Spirit teaches me the wonderful things of God.

I have a new love for people when I leave there.

I am led beside still waters, green meadows, and gardens of love there.

I receive a glimpse of Heaven there.

He always sees me as beautiful there.

He always knows the right thing to say to my heart there.

I never have to prove myself to Him there.

No earthly desire or pleasure compares to spending even one moment there at His feet.

My heart is free there.

When I am sitting at His feet there, I am not hiding from life's problems, but simply seeing them through His eyes.

When all hell seems to be breaking loose in my life, He reminds me there that I am going to make it, because He is my strength.

I am humbled at His feet, because I see the real me.

I can be cleansed from the filth of the world there because of His precious Blood.

Living Loved

It's my get-a-way even when I can't get away.

It's a place to rest my mind, body, soul, and spirit.

His grace surrounds me there.

His power flows through me there.

When I am at His feet, He shows me new areas to overcome, but reminds me that He is always there to help.

He is my Beloved there.

He heals my deepest wounds there at His feet.

Nothing I say to Him ever takes Him by surprise, because He is familiar with all my ways.

His banner over me is love.

He is always waiting for me there and looks forward to when I return.

I can let my heart be free in worship and praise to Him there.

He reminds me there to lift my head up, because where I am weak, He is strong.

The only thing holding me back from daily spending time at His feet is me.

Living Loved

He reminds me to guard what He has entrusted to me there.

I have no past there.

He reminds me to always approach Him as a little child.

I have a better under-standing of what things grieve His heart and what things bring Him joy.

He is never too busy to welcome me to sit at His feet there.

The more time I spend with Jesus, the more time I want to spend with Him.

I cast all my cares on Him there.

It's where feelings are never an indicator of His nearness, because He is always near to me—always.

It's such a gentle, quiet, and peaceful place.

Jesus is proud of me there.

He loves me more than I will ever know!

19

PROMISES AND DECLARATIONS

"God never made a promise that was too good to be true."
D.L. Moody

I compiled these personalized verses for you to use as worship to God, as an encouragement to your heart and as a weapon against the enemy. Read them all often, or grab ahold of one or two, and meditate on them continually until they become part of you. You are loved!

I thank You that You have made ALL things new in my life! (2 Corinthians 5:17)

I only do those things that please my Father today! (John 8:29)

I am complete in Him Who is the Head of all principality and power. (Colossians 2:10)

I am surrounded by a shield of favor. (Psalm 5:12)

I have forsaken all, taken up my cross, and I am following You. (Luke 14:26-33)

I am alive with Christ. (Ephesians 2:5)

My identity is rooted in being loved and being a lover of God! (John 14:21)

I am free from the law of sin and death. (Romans 8:2)

I thank You that as I seek You with all my heart, I will find You! (Jeremiah 29:11-13)

I ask and it shall be given unto me; I seek and I shall find; I knock and it shall be opened to me. (Matthew 7:7,8)

I am far from oppression, and fear does not come near me. (Isaiah 54:14)

I abhor what is evil today, and I cling to that which is good. (Romans 12:9)

I walk in the wisdom of God today. (James 1:5)

You, O Lord, are a shield for me, my glory and the One who lifts up my head. (Psalm 3:3)

I declare today that I love God with ALL my heart, mind, soul and strength. (Luke 10:27)

I walk in the Spirit today, and I do not fulfill the lusts and desires of the flesh. (Galatians 5:16)

You have come that I would have life more abundantly. (John 10:10)

I am born of God, and the evil one does not touch me. (1 John 5:18)

I will not worry today or be anxious. (Philippians 4:6)

I declare that the love of God has been poured out in my heart by the Holy Spirit who was given to me. (Romans 5:5)

I am holy and without blame before Him in love. (1 Peter 1:16; Ephesians 1:4)

I trust in the Lord today with ALL MY HEART, and I do not lean on my own understanding. IN ALL MY WAYS, I will acknowledge Him, and He will direct my paths. (Proverbs 3:5,6)

I will pray without ceasing. (1 Thessalonians 5:17)

I will praise without ceasing! (Psalm 34:1)

I have the mind of Christ. (Philippians 2:5; 1 Corinthians 2:16).

I receive the fullness of God's love today! (Ephesians 3:17-19)

You work ALL THINGS together for good, because I love You, and I am called according to Your purposes. (Romans 8:28)

I have the peace of God that passes all understanding. (Philippians 4:7)

You are keeping me in perfect peace, because my mind is stayed on You. (Isaiah 26:3)

I have the Greater One living in me; greater is He Who is in me than he who is in the world. (1 John 4:4)

I declare today that NOTHING is too hard or impossible for God. (Luke 1:37)

I walk in the strength of the joy of the Lord today. (Nehemiah 8:10)

I declare today that His banner over me is LOVE, LOVE, LOVE! (Song of Songs 2:4)

I call unto the Lord, and He shall answer me and show me great and mighty things! (Jeremiah 33:3)

I walk in the prophetic today. (1 Corinthians 14:1)

I hear the voice of God today. (John 10:4-5)

I walk in divine appointments. (Psalm 37:23)

I have received the gift of righteousness and reign as a king in life through Jesus Christ. (Romans 5:17)

The blessing of God has overtaken me! (Deuteronomy 28:2)

As I wait on the Lord today, my strength is renewed, and I shall mount up with wings like eagles. I shall run and not grow weary, and I shall walk and not faint. (Isaiah 40:31)

This is the day that the Lord has made, and I will rejoice and be glad in it! (Psalm 118:24)

I have received the spirit of wisdom and revelation in the knowledge of Jesus, the eyes of my understanding being enlightened. (Ephesians 1:17,18)

I am CONFIDENT of this very thing, that He who has begun a good work in me will complete it until the day of Jesus Christ. (Philippians 1:6)

I have the tongue of the learned that I should know how to speak a word in season. (Isaiah 50:4)

I walk in the Isaiah 61 mandate today. (Isaiah 61)

I have received the power of the Holy Spirit to lay hands on the sick and see them recover, to cast out demons, and to speak with new tongues. I have power over all the power of the enemy, and nothing shall by any means harm me. (Mark 16:17,18; Luke 10:17,19)

I am free from all condemnation, because I am in Christ Jesus. (Romans 8:1)

I thank You that everything that I set my hand to do is blessed! (Deuteronomy 28:12)

I have put off the old man and have put on the new man, which is renewed in knowledge after the image of Him Who created me. (Colossians 3:9,10)

I put on the whole armor of God today. (Ephesians 6:11-17)

I declare that NO weapon formed against me or my family today will prosper, and every tongue that rises up against us in judgment shall be condemned. (Isaiah 54:17)

I present my body today as a living sacrifice, holy, acceptable to God which is my reasonable service. (Romans 12:1)

I will not be conformed to this world, but I will be transformed by the renewing of my mind. (Romans 12:2)

I have given, and it is given to me; good measure, pressed down, shaken together, and running over, men give into my bosom. (Luke 6:38)

I have NO LACK, because God supplies all my needs according to His riches in glory by Christ Jesus. (Philippians 4:19)

I can quench all the fiery darts of the wicked one with my shield of faith. (Ephesians 6:16)

I can do all things through Christ Jesus who gives me strength. (Philippians 4:13)

I shall do even greater works than Christ Jesus. (John 14:12)

I show forth the praises of God who has called me out of darkness into His marvelous light. (1 Peter 2:9)

I will bless the Lord at ALL times; His praise shall continually be in my mouth. (Psalm 34:1)

I am God's child—for I am born again of the incorruptible seed of the Word of God, which lives and abides forever. (1 Peter 1:23)

I am a person after God's own heart! (Acts 13:22)

I am God's workmanship, created in Christ unto good works. (Ephesians 2:10)

I am a new creature in Christ. (2 Corinthians 5:17)

I am a spirit being—alive to God. (1 Thessalonians 5:23; Romans 6:11)

I am a believer, and the light of the Gospel shines in my mind. (2 Corinthians 4:4)

I declare that my family is debt free! (Philippians 4:19)

I am a doer of the Word, and I am blessed in my actions. (James 1:22,25)

I am a joint-heir with Christ. (Romans 8:17)

I am more than a conqueror through Him who loves me. (Romans 8:37)

I am an overcomer by the blood of the Lamb and the word of my testimony. (Revelation 12:11)

I am a partaker of His divine nature. (2 Peter 1:3,4)

I am an ambassador for Christ. (2 Corinthians 5:20)

I am the righteousness of God in Jesus Christ. (2 Corinthians 5:21)

I am part of a chosen generation, a royal priesthood, a holy nation, a purchased people. (1 Peter 2:9)

I am the temple of the Holy Spirit; I am not my own. (1 Corinthians 6:19)

I am the head and not the tail; I am above only and not beneath. (Deuteronomy 28:13)

I am the light of the world. (Matthew 5:14)

I am the salt of the earth. (Matthew 5:13)

I am His elect, full of mercy, kindness, humility, and longsuffering. (Romans 8:33; Colossians 3:12)

I owe a debt of love to everyone today. (Rom. 13:8)

I am forgiven of ALL my sins and washed in the blood. (Ephesians 1:7; 1 John 1:9)

God has REMOVED my sins as far as the east is from the west. (Psalm 103:12)

I am delivered from the power of darkness and translated into God's kingdom. (Colossians 1:13)

I am redeemed from the curse of sin, sickness, and poverty. (Galatians 3:13; Deuteronomy 28:15-68)

I am firmly rooted, built up, established in my faith, and overflowing with gratitude. (Colossians 2:7)

I am called of God to be the voice of His praise. (2 Timothy 1:9; Psalm 66:8)

I am healed by the stripes of Jesus, and I walk in divine health. (1 Peter 2:24; Isaiah 53:5)

I am raised up with Christ and am seated in heavenly places. (Colossians 2:12; Ephesians 2:6)

I am GREATLY loved by God. (Colossians 3:12; Romans 1:7; 1 Thessalonians 1:4; Ephesians 2:4)

I am strengthened with all might according to His glorious power. (Colossians 1:11)

I am submitted to God, and the devil flees from me, because I resist him in the name of Jesus. (James 4:7)

I am strong in the Lord and in the power of His might. (Ephesians 6:10)

I press on toward the goal to win the prize to which God in Christ Jesus is calling us upward. (Philippians 3:14)

For God has not given me a spirit of fear, but of power, love and a sound mind. (2 Timothy 1:7)

It is not I who live, but Christ lives in me. (Galatians 2:20)

I declare that NOTHING shall separate me from the love of God! (Romans 8:38,39)

I keep myself in the LOVE OF GOD today! (Jude 21)

ABOUT THE AUTHOR

Revive International was founded by Ryan Bruss to take the Gospel of Jesus Christ to the nations of the world. Ryan has had the privilege of traveling to many countries, seeing people saved, healed, and delivered! With a passion for revival and the Father heart of God, he has seen the power of God in salvations, prophecy, and miracles—from house churches to open air meetings. Besides traveling to minister, Ryan, along with an amazing group of passionate believers, pastors a church in North Carolina called Antioch Community Church. Ryan and his beautiful wife, Megan, have been married for over 21 years and have two wonderful kids, Elianna and Andrew.

If you would like Ryan to come and minister, please contact us at: reviveus247@gmail.com or you can visit our websites at: www.reviveus.org or
www.antiochcommunitychurch.org

Other books by Ryan Bruss can be found on Amazon:
How To Encourage Yourself In The Lord

Carrying the Presence: How To Bring The Kingdom Of God To Anyone, Anywhere

Killing Lazarus: Discover Why The Enemy Is Trying To Take Your Out And What You Can Do About It

Living Loved

Printed in Great Britain
by Amazon